THE
DATING
SURVIVAL
GUIDE

**By the same author
and published by Robson Books**

THE BREAK-UP SURVIVAL KIT – Emotional Rescue for the
Newly Single

THE DATING SURVIVAL GUIDE

The Top Ten Tactics for Total Success

Dr Pam Spurr

ROBSON BOOKS

First published in Great Britain in 2002 by
Robson Books, 64 Brewery Road, London N7 9NT

A member of **Chrysalis** Books plc

British Library Cataloguing in Publication Data
A catalogue record for this title is available from
the British Library

ISBN 1 86105 502 1

Typeset by SX Composing DTP, Rayleigh, Essex
Printed by Creative Print and Design (Wales), Ebbw Vale

CONTENTS

To Nick – one hot date!

To my mother and late father for all your
touching, romantic stories

ACKNOWLEDGEMENTS

Thanks to the many women and men who've shared their dating stories with me over the years. Most of us want the same things – romance, love, and to be valued by one special person – we simply take different journeys getting there. When you finally find that special someone to share your life with, you realise what true happiness is.

My warmest thanks to Jeremy Robson for all his encouragement and support. And my thanks also to Jo Brooks and Natalie Jerome.

I'd like to acknowledge that just because this book is aimed at straight women looking for love with straight men, this in no way reflects on the validity and importance of dating in the gay, lesbian, bisexual scene and alternative lifestyle worlds. Those simply require special consideration in terms of added pressures these groups may experience to 'conform' to society's norms. Pressures that hopefully, one day, won't exist!

INTRODUCTION

It's a jungle out there in the world of dating; with hurdles to leap (where's my *very own* Tarzan?); challenges to your self-esteem to contend with (was I dumped because I'm a *plain Jane*?); and many ups and downs. In my years as an agony aunt, life coach and psychologist I've met personally, spoken to, or been in e-mail contact with literally thousands of women on the dating scene. The stories I've heard have ranged from the *usual* – 'He never called for a second date' – to the *surprising* – 'He seemed to be Mr. Perfect, I mean he even talked about marriage, and then I realised he was seeing loads of other women, and men, too!' – to the *shocking* – 'I thought things were great and then realised he was trying to con me into investing money in a business scam!' You may think, 'Oh, I know the feeling,' or 'That poor woman,' but to be completely honest – it can often be their own fault! This is the first thing we all have to accept when getting out on the dating scene. We make the choices: we can choose to see what's actually going on (and it could be good things going on!), or we can close our eyes to reality if things aren't going as planned.

Most women have a way of blinding themselves to the obvious because they try to see *the best* in everyone – even the rogues. Now I'm not saying a bit-of-bad-boy from time to time can't be fun for some casual dating. We've all been there and bad boys sometimes can be fun. They usually have bags of chemistry – but like to spread it around! But hoping the bad boy you've just met is going to change overnight is wishful thinking –

and a waste of your time if you want a romantic relationship.

Equally it's not just bad behaviour from the men that can make dating hazardous to your emotional health but bad behaviour from the women too. Let's take the extremes of dating behaviour. Playing 'hard to get' is good (and I'll explain this clearly in TACTIC THREE) but playing the Ice-Queen and making a man 'hack through the ice' just to get a shred of affection or acknowledgement that he's a bit interesting, can lose you lots of good ones. On the other hand serving yourself up 'for dessert' (need I say more) on your first date – or worse yet when you've just picked someone up randomly on a night out – leads to you being devoured and left feeling as empty inside as an empty dessert plate is on the outside. Not the sort of behaviour to lead to true romance and presumably as you're reading THE DATING SURVIVAL GUIDE you're hoping that dating will lead to romance which will lead on to a relationship. That's why I've written it – to spell out the TEN TACTICS women need to use in order to put their best foot forward; to get control of the dating they do; and to work him out too, as dating material.

Having illustrated two extremes of dating behaviour, I wonder if *you* recognise any of the following sorts of rather *questionable* but more typical behaviour most women get up to when dating. Does hanging by the phone that *never* seems to ring sound familiar? Do you pick it up and check to see if the line's still working? (Yeah right, as if it magically decides to break down when you're waiting for 'Mr. Possibility' to ring. What are the chances of that – one in a million?) Or worse yet, have you been madly 'texting', ringing, and e-mailing the 'Mr. Possibility' with whom you had a couple of dates? He seemed *so keen* so you decided to be liberated and make the next move – only to find, with growing horror, that he seemed to be ignoring you. Yes – you!

In the back of your mind lurks the slight fear that you've crossed into 'stalker/bunny boiler' territory through your rather desperate behaviour. 'What's wrong with *him*?' you wail over a drink to friends. 'He acted like he wanted to see me soon – and nothing, zero!' It then begins to dawn on you it may be a question of, 'What's wrong with *me*?' making you feel somewhat confused about yourself!

Equally disconcerting for your ego – what about getting up false hopes when you meet someone you think could be '*it*', only to have them dashed when you realise just how poor your 'loser-radar' turned out to be? It took two, or maybe ten, dates (wow – practically a relationship nowadays!) before you realised he was 'married' to his mum, only interested in *his* sexual satisfaction, and had truly unmentionable personal habits, but *not* before you'd announced his existence to everyone (and this is the sad reality of e-mail – as you can announce to all your friends instantaneously, that you're on to a hot new 'Mr. Possibility'!). Then just as quickly, you have to *unannounce* this, squirming with embarrassment when people ask you why you changed your mind.

And now for your friends! Do you and your friends spend endless hours going over and over the same ground like: 'Why can't men simply be straight about things?' You all agree that *you'd* be reasonably honest and let a man know if *you* weren't interested, so you wonder how honesty seems to go out the window too easily with them once the dating starts. The cycle goes on and you continue to survive the dating scene – but only just – by holding on to a little bit of hope. Thank goodness we women are optimists – we simply need to channel this optimism in the right way – by getting my TEN TACTICS to work for you!

Soon into the dating game, women realise it's not

what they thought it'd be. I'd bet you £1,000 that when you were a child you believed dating would be *loads* of fun, hugely romantic and exciting. You couldn't wait until you were old enough to date. You practised early, trying on your mum's clothes, smearing on her make-up and teetering in front of a mirror as if before an imaginary boyfriend. You fantasised about picking and choosing dates as if from a box of chocolates, and you believed you'd capture many hearts. As simple as that – it never crossed your mind that you might get a broken heart!

But now you've come down to earth with a bang, realising these childhood fantasies were *fairy tales*, that dating is not one big box of chocolates where you dangle an eager finger in to pick your favourite of the week, and that your dating skills may not be as charismatic and successful as you thought they'd be. I'd like to show you now that good, fun dating is a *skill* and just like any other skill, it needs to be learned, practised, and refined to an art!

At this point you may feel dating has become a minefield riddled with self-doubt, battered confidence, low self-esteem, and even chronic insecurity over your very own level of desirability. Yes, those are the sorts of *feelings* women may end up with once they've been on the dating scene for a few years. Or when they've come out of the cocoon of a relationship and find themselves dating again. It's amazing how quickly we forget dating can be *dire* for our emotional wellbeing when not treated as a skill – that has to be polished up again.

I believe there are a few key reasons why the dating scene has become so complicated today. In the first place, I really do think our mothers and grandmothers had it easier in some ways in earlier generations. Importantly their roles were much more clear. It was simple – men *were* men and women *were* women! Men were supposed to do all the asking and set the pace for a potential romance. Women were supposed to allow men to take this lead and subtly encourage it. You two met, he took your number, he rang, and you went out together. All things being well, he rang for a second date and you went out again. And so the cycle continued. There were pressures of course – men and women back then wanted to put their best foot forward, make a good match, and fall in love. But once dating was initiated the course of events took a familiar and expected path.

Don't get me wrong – I don't think we should go back to the 'good old days' because there were lots of things to improve on back then – like equal rights. However the land is now muddied, as it never was then. Many men don't want to seem 'aggressive' so they hold back waiting for signals of *her* interest, or for her to do the asking. Many women want to be more confident, take the dating lead, and ask men out, but still have lingering worries that they'll seem too 'forward'. So they send out confusing signals – making it worse for the guy watching for her signals! Get my point?

We also live in an 'instant society' where we can get everything from pizza to home-loans quickly, instantly even, just by picking up the phone or going on line. We have instant access to practically everything including things relating to the dating game. We can go on chat lines, join agencies or as in the old-fashioned way, in person to meet people.

Being surrounded by a quick-fix society, we expect things like romance to happen quickly too. The slow-burn, build-up of yesteryear has been replaced by no one blinking an eye at first-date-sex or at least fairly snap decisions over whether someone's date-material or not. When we don't take time to get to know someone (and *they're* not giving us time) we do miss a lot of good 'Mr Possibilities'. We also leave ourselves open to shallow encounters that quite frankly taint us, leaving us devaluing romance, sex, and relationships generally – casting a dark cloud over our future chances.

Finally we are all guilty of expecting 'it all'. We have bought in to the media myth and social pressure that the people we date should be:

a.   attractive
b.   confident
c.   have a terrific sense of humour
d.   successful
e.   fantastic with our friends
f.   charming to our mums
g.   'manly' with our dads
h.   intelligent
i.   sensitive to our moods
j.   *sensational* with our needs
k.   respect us
l.   be our equal but not be a wimp (tall order!)
m.   stylish
and, of course let's not forget, *solvent*!

There's no room for human 'error' any more! We seek perfection even though we know deep down that we ourselves are not perfect. No one is! Setting these unrealistic targets makes dating even harder – we write one man off the list because he seems a bit shy around our friends (ever thought your friends might be as approachable as a snarling pack of wolves and it'd take nerves of steel to cope with them?). We write off another as he doesn't make much money (despite the fact he loves his work and beams confidently throughout the day). And so it goes on as we write off some really worthy ones, because they don't have the A to Z of our romantic checklist.

I think I've made my point now. Each one of us needs

tactics to survive dating and the feelings, behaviours and modern issues we have to contend with. I'm done with the preaching now, so on with the fun! Yes, fun and excitement, too! Because dating should be a fun adventure and an exciting journey of discovery about ourselves and the people we date.

I've written THE DATING SURVIVAL GUIDE to address the most important dating issues *and more* – so that you can refine your dating skills, employ my TEN TACTICS and win! These tactics are aimed at dating success, *not* at changing you into some sort of pre-packaged perfect date – how boring it would be if we were all the same. They're aimed at enhancing what you've already got (because everyone has a spark of potential) and opening your eyes to the blind spots we all have when it comes to love and romance. Time to get to grips with those tactics.

TACTIC 1: BE ...

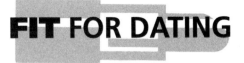

FIT FOR DATING

Because it IS survival of the fittest

There's stiff competition out there for all the great guys – *as well* as the rest of them – which is why dating is such a jungle. We're animals at heart trying to carve out our own patch. We slip on our dating camouflage by putting on a brave face, when trembling inside and playing out our party piece for each new date – only the fit survive in these circumstances. My very first tactic has to do with what I call your 'dating fitness'. This is all about 'prepping' for *starting* dating from a positive point of view. I'm not talking 'first impressions' here – that's covered in TACTIC TWO and very important – don't get ahead of yourself with eagerness!

Dating can be really fun, exhilarating even! But as I pointed out in the introduction it can also leave you miserable and demoralised – usually from the knock backs. Every single one of us gets knock backs. It's *surviving* these through your *responses* to them that indicates your dating fitness. And I want to make sure your fitness is high!

People who have high levels of dating fitness are those who pick themselves up, dust themselves off, and come back for more. They're the ones who win in the game of love. Those who realise that it will come right in the end, get *more* dates, *enjoy* them and *find* their 'Mr. Possibility' ('Mr. P.' here on in) or two! It's all about *learning* from knock backs and not taking them *personally* – unless you deserve it (more on that later!). But what sort of qualities do these 'fittest' people have who'll *survive* the dating game?

⭐ They're 'realists' not die-hard romantics. Less likely to see things through rose-coloured specs means they can think objectively about supposed 'rejection'.

⭐ They have at least moderate confidence, so a knock back isn't the end of the world.

⭐ They're optimists – they know there'll be other date-opportunities around the corner.

⭐ They learn easily from situations, take away this knowledge and use it positively.

⭐ They attract enough fresh offers/interest because people *fancy* people who seem 'centred', 'grounded', and 'fit'.

If you're not like the above (and many of you reading this won't feel like that!) let's put this in perspective. At some point *you* must have knocked back someone who asked you out. Maybe even after having a couple of dates with them you decided not to pursue it further. Now the person (or people) you've knocked back wasn't a 'pathetic loser' was he? Well O.K., he *may* have been, but on the whole you've probably knocked a man back simply because he wasn't your type. *Or* he was looking for a different sort of relationship from the one you wanted. *Or* it even seemed like a good thing for the first few dates but after that, for whatever reason, you lost interest.

Does this reflect badly on him? Not at all! He may have been a bit hurt, surprised, even put out, but thinking about it rationally he'd hopefully come to the conclusion that it simply wasn't meant to be – either the timing, conflicting interests, or work got in the way. Hopefully he realised that someone else around the corner will be gagging to go out with him. Whatever the result you didn't want him to take it personally, and so you too must learn to be resilient and 'fit' in this way. You must put knock backs into perspective.

DATING SURVIVAL STRATEGY: PUTTING KNOCK BACKS INTO PERSPECTIVE

Time to get your pens out – and keep them handy for the rest of THE DATING SURVIVAL GUIDE!

The last knock back I got was: (e.g. six months ago when the new guy I fancied at work wasn't interested)

....

....

I responded by: (e.g. feeling really embarrassed, obsessed about what was wrong with me, etc.)

....

....

In retrospect I could have put it in perspective by: (e.g. realising he felt uncomfortable with work place romances *generally* – particularly being new to the office!)

....

....

My new motto for knock backs: (e.g. if someone doesn't want to go out with me I'll think 'it's their loss NOT mine!' or 'their choice does NOT reflect on me personally!')

....

....

In doing this Dating Survival Strategy and putting knock backs *into perspective* you'll build your confidence and increase your dating fitness. And fitness means you can keep throwing yourself back into dating even if you've been disappointed by someone's response – or lack of it. That's what happened with Sophie.

When I first met Sophie her dating confidence was on the floor – absolutely rock bottom. The last three men she'd been interested in had not returned her interest, or at least her *level* of interest. Now she'd sworn off men and said she wanted to concentrate on making some career changes. Sophie came to me for 'life coaching' with a view to identifying and enhancing her various professional skills.

As an aside Sophie threw into our first conversation the fact that her career was now all-important as she'd 'given up' on men. This immediately grabbed my interest. Why was she giving up on men? She was an interesting, attractive young woman – but obviously she didn't think so! Sophie explained how the last three men she'd met hadn't been interested in carrying on dating for the following reasons: Dave didn't want to get serious having just come out of a long-term relationship; Jonathon was moving out of the city and didn't want a long distance relationship; and Richard only wanted casual dating as his work was really taking off.

Thought about rationally these knock backs didn't reflect on Sophie *personally*. But she *chose* to see them this way. Sophie felt that if she'd *been* a 'good catch',

Dave would've wanted to get serious with her; ditto for Jonathon who would've been prepared to give a long distance relationship a try; and ditto again – Richard would have believed Sophie was special enough to be equal to work.

Once I had Sophie put these into perspective she saw it wasn't that *she was undesirable* but that she'd simply had a run of bad dating luck.

__CAUTION ALERT!__ (Occasionally I'll qualify what I've just written with a 'caution alert' as in certain circumstances the opposite of what's generally true may be operating – so you need to consider whether the alert applies to you.)

Sometimes though, 'bad luck' actually turns out to be a *subconscious desire* to choose a certain type of man – what I call an '*un*-man'– e.g. *un*available, *un*reliable, or *un*attached for a good reason – no one wants him! More on that though, in TACTIC SEVEN – Sort the Princes From Frogs. This was not the case with Sophie who'd had lots of dating success in the past – a good sign your subconscious isn't putting you into *un*workable dating situations.

DATING SURVIVAL STRATEGY: YOU HAVE CHOICES!

Just as Sophie had made the *choice* that she was *not* a good catch, after our chat about putting knock backs in perspective, she *chose* to believe it was circumstance, not her, that meant she didn't date any of those three men.

__My new choice:__ (Write yours down, e.g. 'I'm going to choose *NOT* to find the negative but *look for* the positive reasons behind things!'):

....

....

Making such choices ensures you are *fit to survive* the dating game!

What happened to Sophie brings me to another point that will build your dating fitness to keep going and enjoy the dating game. This is the issue of 'Romantic Trade-offs'. Everyone uses 'trade-offs' in dating and relationships and if you can *understand* yours – and a potential date's trade-offs – it will enhance your experiences.

Romantic trade-offs are quite literally the 'chips' you use to play the dating game. It's what you 'give' when you first meet someone, and what you expect back in return. You may be prepared to make a trade-off, e.g., seeing less of your friends in order to see *more* of 'Mr. P.'. Women do this particular trade-off much more frequently than men – giving up friends in the name of potential romance. They're also more likely to make trade-offs earlier on that really impact on their lives. These trade-offs occur more often for women perhaps because on the whole our self-esteem is more bound up with dating. Many women's self-esteem is lower when they're not dating anyone and higher when they are. And if you give big trade-offs (like ignoring your friends while you desperately hang on to his every word) and don't get much in return (he goes on a date with you when it suits him), you'll eventually take an emotional battering.

I've got to hand it to men, on the other hand, who tend to find more of a balance. Their trade-offs are more subtle, taking the form of, e.g. 'I'll ring her more frequently than I usually do', or 'I'll take her to that restaurant she loves even though I don't like Chinese food'. You'll rarely find them giving up a night out with friends for you – at least as early on as women will. Once they're more sure of their feelings for you they may make such a trade-off.

The trade-offs you're prepared to make often reflect

your level of confidence when it comes to men. The
more *frequent* and *far-reaching* trade-offs you make
early on, the more likely you are simply aiming to please
potential dates – probably because you feel they won't
be interested otherwise. I'm sure we've all been guilty of
this from time to time!

DATING SURVIVAL STRATEGY: TRADE-OFFS I MAKE/HAVE MADE
In the past I've made these sorts of trade-offs: (e.g.
Put my other friends second)

....

....

These have resulted in: (e.g. I've lost some friendships)

....

....

In future I won't use the following trade-offs: (e.g.
I won't neglect friendships for dates)

....

....

I hope analysing the trade-offs you've made in the
past will increase your dating fitness, and that in future
you won't make any confidence-draining, self-esteem
lowering trade-offs! When you're making good choices
and reasonable trade-offs it shows in your whole person
– you become more resilient and confident (but more of
this in TACTIC TWO – Be Fantastic at First Impressions.
I'll probably repeat this a few times in THE DATING
SURVIVAL GUIDE – but confidence **is attractive!**

When you deserve a knock back:
I mentioned earlier there are times when a person
deserves knock backs because of their dating behaviour.

If you're doing pretty much *any* of the following then you're likely to get some knock backs and deserve them! Sorry, but that's the truth and if we're going to improve your dating fitness, you need to face it.

- On the first date you talk on and on about recent dating 'horrors'
- You clearly ask if your date is looking for a relationship/marriage
- You drink too much and make a complete fool of yourself
- You throw yourself at your date (scary – even for a man!)
- You ask overly personal/intimate questions
- You moan about how horrible it is being single (the implication being that seeing this man for a date is pretty horrible too!)
- You make your 'romantic checklist' very obvious and seem to be mentally checking things off *about him* as the evening wears on
- You drone on about your ex-boyfriend

Have you done any of the above *or similar*?   YES/NO

Write down here the thing you've done that deserved a knock back:

....

....

I think you get my meaning. The above behaviour will not improve your dating survival chances. Once you've focused on these you'll be able to guard against them in the future.

This quiz is a quick indicator of your dating fitness.

   CAUTION ALERT! *Only* honest answers will help *you*!

**1.   Someone you fancy turns you down for a
        date – are you most likely to:**
a.   Worry about why he didn't fancy you
b.   Cry and/or feel really down about it
c.   Shrug your shoulders and get on with it

**2.   Friends want to set you up on a blind date –
        how do you respond:**
a.   Go depending on how much you trust their
      judgement to make a good match
b   Feel you must be very 'sad' *OR* desperate to grab
      any chance of a date
c.   Go along thinking – 'what's a girl got to lose?'

3.   Would you ever ask a guy out?
a.   I'd worry what they'd think – it would have to be
      exceptional circumstances
b.   I've jumped in and asked loads of guys out
c.   Definitely in the right circumstances

4.   Where does flirting come in to dating?
a.   I worry about when to, or not to, flirt
b.   It's the *only* way to communicate
      interest/attraction
c.   Flirting is one way to let people know they're a
      little special

THE DATING FITNESS QUIZ KEY
**3 or 4 Cs – Fantastic Fitness – you're heading for
dating survival!**
The C answers reflect flexibility on your part. The fittest

people when it comes to surviving dating are those who can judge each situation on its merit – they're flexible. They don't have one blanket rule for how to act, and they're quite optimistic with a 'go for it' attitude (see question no. 3). That said, they don't 'go for it' by leaping in without thought (answer 'b' question 3).

3 or 4 As – OK Fitness – you'll survive dating – but only just! (Of course you get a pretty good fitness rating if your other choices were Cs.)

I think you'd agree with me that you lack confidence in terms of how to handle the dating scene. There's a certain tentativeness about your dating behaviour. Analyse your last few dates – or knock backs – in terms of how you could've been more positive. With hindsight some things are obvious. But it's important to take this knowledge to the next level and avoid these in the future while emphasising the fitness you have.

3 or 4 Bs – Poor Fitness – dating survival chances = low!

Oops – you've got to watch out. You need to take all the advice in TACTIC ONE seriously. To be fit you need to take knock backs 'like a woman', you need to be able to make good choices and avoid any extremes of dating behaviour. Consider the following:

TACTIC ONE POINTERS:

> **Knock backs:** Ouch! It hurts you when you get a knock back. You've got to remind yourself of the DATING SURVIVAL STRATEGIES above – dealing with knock backs and your choices.
> **Blind dates:** Friends usually try and make sensible choices for blind dates. If you have fantastic fitness you'll recognise this and go along to make your own judgement without making a big issue

of it. If your dating fitness isn't that high you tend to read too much into blind date invitations – like 'how sad do they think I am!' Accept invitations with an open mind.

Asking men out: There's nothing wrong with asking a guy out but it's how you do it, and what you follow it with, that counts in dating survival. Flexible awareness allows you to judge whether the man you've just met would be flattered to be asked out, or whether you need to 'coax' a date out of him. Try saying something vague but optimistic like, 'It'd be great to get together sometime,' allowing him then to do the asking.

Flirting: Flirting is great – it feels good. But there's flirting and overdoing it by throwing yourself at someone or never being able to turn your flirt switch off. Try to vary the amount of flirting you do. When you catch yourself saying the third flirtatious thing running, change tack and perhaps try choosing a more serious topic of conversation. Much more on flirting in TACTICs TWO and FOUR.

The most important thing I've learned from TACTIC ONE is:

....

....

And I'm not going to forget this!

TACTIC 2:
BE ...

FANTASTIC at first impressions

Survive first impressions and first dates!

I cannot stress to you enough how much first impressions count. It's a bit of an over-optimistic, romantic urban myth that you *can* turn things around if you don't catch someone's eye straight off. It's *possible*, but it actually takes a great deal of effort to change first impressions. Psychologists have found that within the first *few seconds* we make up our minds about a person's physical attractiveness, followed swiftly by judgements about their background, social status and personality. Are we amazingly *quick* to judge, or what?

You're probably not surprised that we're quick to judge physical attributes – you're either attracted to someone's appearance or not. But all that other stuff – personality, background – to boot? Well let me explain. Humans are essentially lazy creatures of habit, so it makes us feel comfortable to *stereotype* people. If in the past we've come across a blonde in a short skirt who *was* a good-time girl we tend to judge the next blonde the same. If our last boyfriend was a lawyer *and* controlling, we assume all lawyers are controlling.

So the process goes on – particularly when we're judging someone's romantic potential. We extrapolate from the physical, the body language a person gives off, the clothes they've chosen, their profession, and finally when they first open their mouth – their accent, vocal tone, speech content, and conversational ability. And all this is done with computer-like speed.

Don't be demoralised at this point because there's so much you can *do* with first impressions to make them work for you! I simply want you to be *aware* of the importance of first impressions. Awareness is a great weapon with which to arm yourself to make the most of opportunities. Looks are what impacts first, *but* men being the creatures they are, often hover *undecided* on whether they find you their fantasy dream-girl or not. They *do* give us a chance to send out more signals to give them a basis for making a final decision – probably more chances than we women give them! *While* they're hovering about this decision it's crucial to turn every signal you're giving off to your advantage. This TACTIC is about covering the main bases for making your first impression count, giving you the very best start.

Also, this doesn't apply to people who've gone through the experience of 'growing on' each other. We've all known couples who started as friends or work colleagues, got on well, shared interests and relied on each other, too. Then one night (usually after a drink or two – the power of alcohol to unleash unspoken desire!) they found themselves kissing and from there, friendship became romance. For these couples first impressions didn't count! They were long past that stage when romantic feelings began to blossom.

So given that most of us stereotype people quickly (in dating this means being slotted into 'potential date/mate material' versus 'not for me' categories), how can we make the most of first impressions? Here in TACTIC TWO I'll give you the *building blocks* for making great first impressions. It's *very practical* so it'll be easy for you to put into practice – no excuses! And the good thing about starting practically is that it continues the good work from TACTIC ONE in kick-starting your *confidence*. You're going to swim through TACTIC TWO and think, 'Hmm, I'm going to get really good at this!' We'll move on to trickier topics in coming TACTICS.

WHEN FIRST IMPRESSIONS ACTUALLY *START*

First impressions begin from a number of points. Maybe you're being set up on a blind date. The friend arranging it will give a run-down of your main points to the other – giving you both a pre-conceived image of what the other is like. Perhaps you've bumped into someone at a work conference or who's visiting your office for a meeting – first impressions will already be gaining pace. First impressions can begin in a crowded bar, a friend's party, a lift, the supermarket, your gym, etc., where you exchange phone numbers and arrange to meet up.

* CAUTION ALERT!* If you meet a stranger in any of these or similar ways, ensure you take *their* number rather than give them yours, only arrange daytime dates in public places (e.g. not some lonely park), and tell friends where you're going and who you're meeting. Most of you will probably take such precautions but I come across too many women who are too trusting.

Such first impressions are spontaneous and therefore have a slightly different set of 'dating survival strategies' compared to when you enter the territory of *an actual first date*. Let's deal with these first by the following:

SPONTANEOUS MEETINGS/INTRODUCTIONS – DATING SURVIVAL STRATEGIES:

As you can't plan when such spontaneous meetings will happen, the best you can do is *prepare* yourself, knowing at some point one *might* occur. Here's a *simple* list of things that will make a spontaneous meeting a positive experience for you and 'Mr. P.' Whether you catch his eye over the frozen foods in your local supermarket (believe me this does happen!) or he walks into your office, try the following mini-tactics. Research shows *most* people meet their future partners in such chance encounters – it's more likely than your friends successfully setting you up.

♥ Raise yourself up either in your seat or where standing, by pulling your shoulders back and neck straight. Good posture quite simply looks *confident*. Confidence *is attractive*. If you slouch you look like you're 'hiding' something. We'll come to the fuller range of dating body language a bit later in this chapter.

♥ If you're a 'leg-swinger' (someone who crosses their legs and then keeps swinging the top one as if it was a pendulum) – stop it! It makes you look tense. Plant your feet on the floor to stop yourself slipping into this bit of body language that shrieks 'nervous!'

♥ Equally for 'nail pickers' who start fiddling with their nails/cuticles the moment they feel awkward – don't do it! It *doesn't* shout 'confidence!' Clasp your hands together to prevent it, or slip them casually onto your hips if you're standing – very inviting to the male eye as it draws their line of vision to the curve of your hips.

♥ Smile openly. When you smile you look relaxed and approachable. I'd be *rich* if I had a pound for every time a man has told me, 'She was attractive but simply didn't look *approachable*.'

♥ Visualise someone you're comfortable with – your best friend or mum, even. Thinking of a 'comforting' person will immediately relax you and you'll feel less nervous with this 'Mr. P.' who's just crossed your path. Even if your very first panicky thought was, 'God he's gorgeous – what do I *say*, what do I *do*?'

♥ Keep it simple when you *open* your mouth, you're much less likely to get tongue-tied. For example, if you're in an office scenario ask 'Mr. P.' if you 'can help with something'. If you're at the frozen foods make some comment about 'selecting from the vast array of choices'. Such open ended, straightforward comments *ask* for a response without being threatening – i.e. you won't come across as a stalker!

♥ Start some *simple* flirting – serious flirting comes later. A 'head-dip' à la the late Princess Diana is subtle but provocative. She was famous for looking up from under her fringe. Tilting your chin toward your chest you look up with eyes *directly* into 'Mr. P's' face. Sounds old fashioned but, hey, you're appealing to his ancestral genes!

♥ Another subtle flirty message is to lean in slightly towards 'Mr. P.' This brings your personal spaces closer together but is not as inviting as 'The Bridge' (that comes later).

♥ A good old-fashioned giggle at anything 'Mr. P.' says that's *remotely* funny is also a small flirty icebreaker.

♥ Now if he seems to be responding favourably – look for smiles, small talk, little jokes, and posture that starts to relax – you're starting to get somewhere positive with this first impression.

Closing the deal – Now's the tricky part. You've both been thrown together by chance and have entered into realms of 'possibility'. By this I mean you're both in a bit of a stand-off, 'sussing out' whether the other's interested by how much you've given away in terms of subtle flirting behaviour and small talk. Both of you (or maybe only one of you) is wondering where this is leading – is there a possibility of a date? And believe me 99.9% of single men and women (and sadly too many *attached* ones too!) will be thinking about the chances of a date, coffee, drink, or whatever you want to call it, in these sorts of situations. I know because they tell me so!

If you're interested in 'closing the deal' and seeing this 'Mr. P.' again, wait a moment to see if he asks for your number. If he doesn't, but seems hesitant to leave, you should feel free to ask for his, or at least orchestrate 'closing the deal' by saying something that applies to the situation. For example in a supermarket encounter, 'We seem to have lots in common in terms of our frozen food choices . . . maybe we should compare fruit and veg choices.' Because this is one of the situations where some modern men worry about doing the wrong thing and getting knocked back. If you're feeling confident simply suggest, with a smile and in a straightforward way, 'Why don't we have a coffee one day?' (Recall from TACTIC ONE – there's nothing wrong with asking a man out, it's simply *how you do it*! Act like you've already decided he's great-*mate* material and you'll scare him off. Act like you're a busy confident person, but you've got space to see him, and he'll be pleased (and then let him do the asking for the second date!).

If this doesn't get the desired response – a date – chalk it up to experience. There's *nothing* lost but everything to gain from such a result. You've shown you can smile and ask a straight question without doing the things we all dread – freezing up, giggling hysterically, or gabbling on incoherently. Good practice for you even if this 'Mr. P.' didn't want a date!

YOUR MOST RECENT CHANCE ENCOUNTER

I'd like you now to think about a chance encounter you had recently where you fancied the man involved – what happened?

When was your last chance encounter with a 'Mr. P.'?

....

....

What was the outcome of this encounter?

....

....

Did you by chance do any of the suggestions above?

....

....

Can you now see anything you'd do differently?

....

....

FIRST DATE TACTICS – THE IMPRESSION YOU GIVE:

Now let's turn to the all-important first date, where first impressions count a great deal. These can be make or break situations which is why TACTIC TWO is so important. But at least you've got the edge over a chance encounter as you've *secured* the date and can allow it to unfold under *your control*. I'm going to break this into four easy pieces – (1) *Before* the date; (2) *Approaching* the date; (3) *During* the date; and (4) *The end* of the date.

1. Before the date

It's arranged now – how can you *best* prepare? Here are the main bases to cover:

 Visualise – Each day leading up to the date, take a few moments to visualise how successful it's going to be. See yourself smiling, acting confidently, taking things in your stride. You flirt, you laugh and have fun – all the things a good date's supposed to be. So you think you'll feel foolish doing this? Just think of the multi-million-pound-earning athletes who use this technique – footballers visualise scoring goals, tennis players visualise serving aces, etc., to great success. Why shouldn't daters visualise?

 Motto – Any time you catch nerve-wracking thoughts creeping into your mind, substitute them with a positive motto, e.g., 'No matter what happens I'll enjoy myself!' Write yours here:

....

....

You *are* what you think!

 Affirmation – Think about your three best points. Put them on a post-it note inside your bathroom cabinet or desk drawer – somewhere you'll catch sight of them each day. *Believe* them! You've got these qualities *and more* to offer someone.

....

....

 Early preparation – Think about what would be suitable to wear. Don't leave it to *the* night when you run around in a panic slinging outfit after outfit onto the floor – working up a *lovely sweat* even though you've already showered and are due to leave for the date in minutes! Sounds familiar? I've been there and it's no way to start a first date! You may *love* your slinky black dress but if you're meeting at a pub for a drink it'll simply look OTT. A couple of days beforehand try on suitable things and select the outfit that both suits the venue and is one in which you feel *confident*. Let's say you've got a fab top you love wearing out with friends but you have to suck your stomach in the whole time. You want to be *comfortable* on a first date – so choose something just as fab without such problems! Get a guy-pal's opinion. Nothing better than checking out a first-date outfit with a male friend. They're simply more honest than your girl friends probably will be.

__CAUTION ALERT!__ It's one thing to meet someone by chance when you're out clubbing dressed in raunchy club-wear (I've got nothing against club-wear and have been known to enjoy some skimpy outfits myself!) but it's another to go out on a planned first date like that. Stick to a skimpy top and a *less* revealing skirt or vice versa. One or the other! But it's a fact that if you dress for a first date in a *completely* sexy outfit, he's going to think you're after a shallow encounter. If however you are only after a shallow encounter, that's fine – dress for sex.

2. Approaching the date

💗 **Deep breathing** – As you near the moment – about to open the door to the wine bar or wherever you're meeting him – take a few deep breaths and release them *slowly*. With your breathing under control you'll feel less panicked.

💗 **Panic Buddy** – Some friends make us feel great – they always know the right thing to say. If you're nervous give your 'panic buddy' a ring and get a quick pep talk.

- ♥ **Re-affirm both your motto and self-affirmation** – Clearing your head of negative thinking will help maintain your calm. If your mind is racing with frantic thoughts like, 'What if I say something stupid?' the fear will show in your eyes. Remind yourself of your motto and affirmations.

- ♥ **Topic preparation** – For those reading this who are *very shy* and tend to run out of conversation – think about a couple of easy topics to throw into the mix. Remind yourself of the last book you read, video you rented, or film you saw – use these to keep things flowing during the date. You'll be able to ask if he's read, rented, or seen them.

- ♥ **Make your entry** – Better a few minutes late than early. Early does look *too keen*! Stand tall – no point in apologising for your existence with slumped shoulders. Smile broadly, reach for their hand, or be ready if they go to peck your cheek. Being aware of which way they're headed (hand or cheek) will stop any awkward bumping of noses.

3. During the date

Nonverbal communication – body language!
Your body language – It depends how much you like him as to how you use your body language. If things are looking good, try the following to give off a positive and approachable message:

1. 'The Bridge' (mentioned earlier) – Touch his forearm or knee gently with your hand as you make a point, drawing your personal spaces

together. This begins to show you want to exclude the rest of the world.

2. Lightly flick back your hair as if to say, 'Look at me!' It's playful and flirty and shows you *want* his attention.

3. Draw your finger lightly from your neck towards your cleavage. Pause at your upper breastbone. This signals you want him to notice your femininity.

4. If you're standing at a bar the same applies to gently placing a hand on your hip as mentioned earlier.

5. Lean in to him when he says something – as if you only have 'ears' for him.

6. Allow your gaze to linger longer on his face throughout your conversation.

7. 'The Twist' – This gives out a flirty message. Keep your upper body pivoted toward him and pivot your lower body away. It gives out a flirty mixed signal (part of you turned towards but part of you turned away as if you're 'hard to get') that'll drive his subconscious mad.

8. 'The Slide' – If you *really* fancy him, occasionally slide your fingers up and down your drink glass slowly. Slowly is suggestive. Quickly and frequently speaks nerves!

9. 'The Screen' – Leaning in towards him with your shoulders as if to screen the two of you off from other activity gives the message that you're only interested in him.

10. Women with high confidence try not to 'cheapen' their value with overtly strong body language. This is achieved subconsciously but can be 'learned'. For example, there's a difference between letting your finger linger on your breastbone and allowing it to stray further to between the

cleavage. Also gently placing one hand on a hip represents high confidence but allowing your hands to move lower towards the buttocks signals 'easy/available'. More on availability in TACTIC FOUR – Be Sexy Not Easy!

11. If you two really fancy each other you'll find body mirroring going on – where your subconscious takes over and you both mirror the other's movements in subtle ways.

'Mr. P.s' Body Language –

1. Watch out for him doing 'The Bridge', 'The Twist', 'The Slide' or 'The Screen', as men use these pieces of body language, too.

2. Men will draw your eye downwards to their hips (yes, this *is* suggestive!) by looping a finger or thumb in their belt loop.

3. 'The Throat Clear' – When about to say something that subconsciously is getting on personal territory (showing more than likely they're interested) many men will do a brief throat clear. This gives them a moment to build confidence to tackle this area. For example, if they want to find out how recently you had a relationship.

4. Watch out for 'The Saunter' – this is that male way of swaggering when they either fancy you (great!) or think they're on to an *easy thing* (what message have you been giving off girl?)!

5. If as the evening progresses he seems to use a whole body 'Screen', then he's really interested. This is more than a shoulder 'Screen' – his subconscious wants to protect you from the attention of others – the competition.

6. When walking together (to your table, etc.) if he 'Bridges' to either your arm or your lower back he

again is positively interested.

7. Men and their hair presents a slightly different picture from women and their hair. A long stroke suggests he's interested. But a 'flick' suggests he's impatient.

8. Lingering looks – you know when you feel a man's assessing your potential – the way they can look you up and down. Well, they *are* assessing your potential. And they're not being completely shallow looking at your physical attributes – they also pick up your body language cues. So if he gives you the once-over more than once during the date he's fine-tuning his overall first impression – that's a good sign! You're winning the battle. Unless of course as the date's worn on *you've* lost interest.

When 'Mr. P.' Is NOT Interested –

1. If he seems to eye up every other woman who enters the room – sorry – you haven't won him over. His subconscious mind is wandering to what he may be missing.

2. If he asks a question and then doesn't seem to listen to your answers. Either he's not interested but is going through the motions of asking about you. Or he's self-centred and never listens to anyone – you wouldn't want to go out with him anyway!

3. If he clasps his hands behind his head when answering your questions he's anxious about either the topic or giving you a straight answer.

4. If he rarely holds your eye contact during conversation then he's either not interested, or uncomfortable.

5. If he's turned his body side on to you (*not* 'The Twist') during the evening, then he's losing interest fast!

6. If he fails to close the psychological 'Bridge'
    between you and doesn't reach out for any
    contact to draw your personal spaces together.
7. If he leans away from you during conversation –
    he literally wants to keep his distance.
    CAUTION ALERT! Some people are so
    overwhelmed by nerves (yes, your company is *that*
    staggering!) that it becomes hard to read their
    body language. Usually you can tell through
    excess perspiration (what a lovely give away!) and
    a pinched voice that it's nerves and not an
    overwhelming desire to escape your company.

There are some *out of touch* people around who'll want to rain on your 'dating' parade. Usually through a misguided sense of being politically correct they pour scorn on anything like flirting or paying attention to body language. They're simply out of touch with the rest of us who *want* fun, romance, and to feel emotionally connected to someone special. Who enjoy a bit of flirting and hope a good date will turn into another, and another! Let's just let them get on with it shall we?

Spoken communication – conversation – a few Dos and Don'ts!
This part of TACTIC TWO is about getting that extra edge on the first impressions and dates. We've covered First Date body language, so now it's time to give you a list to absorb of *conversational* Dos and Don'ts.

1. Do use that 'emergency' list of topics for when you feel your mind seizing up with nerves. People are happy to talk about films, etc. and such conversations naturally lead on to others.
2. Do allow for occasional pauses in the conversation. There's nothing wrong with that.

It's the uncomfortable silences that go on for more than ten seconds that you've got to watch out for.

3.   Do put the spotlight on him. By asking him about his work, hobbies, etc., the spotlight comes off you until you're more relaxed.

4.   Do remember this is not about being 'the best conversationalist', it's simply about having fun and getting to know him a little. To see if *you* want to go out with *him*!

5.   Do spread the conversation around. Talk about your friends, workmates, hobbies, etc., because if you focus exclusively on one topic (maybe the one you feel most comfortable with) you may come across as boring!

6.   Don't talk about your 'ex'.

7.   Don't ask about his 'ex'.

8.   Don't ask what he's 'looking for in a relationship'. Sounds desperate – i.e. is he looking for someone like you? This fascinating topic you're dying to know the answer to, can come in later dates.

9.   Equally, don't list what you're looking for.

10. Don't ask why he's single – it can sound a bit rude.

11. Don't drone on about problems at work, fights with friends, family rifts – you'll sound like a very negative person!

There! That's the most important list for starters.

4. Ending the date

⭐ If you've had a good time – say so! You don't have to gush about it being the most wonderful date you've ever had, but men need a little encouragement to ask you out again. Keep it simple – 'I had fun,' will do.

★ Seal it with a goodnight kiss – *not* getting your kit off! See TACTIC FOUR for more on this hot topic. Smile and be *approachable* (remember how rich I'd be . . .) so he'll feel comfortable about asking you out again.

If he asks you out again – leave a two-day gap. Don't be available the next day no matter how much you want to be. This *isn't* about game playing as some dating 'experts' would have you believe – it's about staying a little level-headed when your hormones have started rushing passionately around your body! More on this in TACTIC FIVE.

CAUTION ALERT! If he's not concerned about how you're getting home, i.e., safely, then forget him. *People* should be concerned about how others get home. Your mates worry don't they, when you've all been out on the town and you're going separate ways? You want each other to be safe – so should a date! And if you're bigger than him, you should worry about his safety!

A FEW LAST *CRITICAL* POINTS FOR TACTIC TWO!

✔ As I explained under 'body language' – drawing your two personal spaces together is a turn-on. But continual touching and snuggling up too close makes for a bad first impression. Too needy or a bit floozy-like!

✔ Don't drink too much. Honestly if you think using alcohol will cure your nerves, it may do so – but at the same time you may slur your words, say something you regret, make *bad* decisions, or act silly – far worse than a few nerves.

✔ Nerves are to be expected on first dates. Don't act touchy, aloof, or stand-offish if you've been a bit nervous – instead be straightforward or even self- deprecating about it. Nothing wrong with saying, 'I've been a little nervous – things haven't gone quite as I planned. Maybe I need to practise having another first date!'

A *final* word to bear in mind –

If on that first date (or even the second) it's obviously not going to blossom into romance, you may salvage a 'friendship' from the experience. It can be disappointing if you wanted more from your 'Mr. P.' (as you fancied the impression he gave off!) but, hey, there's nothing wrong with adding the occasional new guy-pal to your circle of friends.

The most important thing I've learned from TACTIC TWO is:

....

....

And I'm not going to forget this!

TACTIC 3:
BE ...

CONFIDENT – avoid the 'I'm Unworthy Complex'!

Confidence is *critical* to your dating success. I can assure you this is an absolute truth! Recent films exemplify this perfectly. Think of 'Bridget Jones' – as her confidence increased she was able to make the right choice in terms of men, by the end of the film – choosing her true love Mark Darcy. How about Julia Roberts in 'The Runaway Bride' *and* 'Notting Hill'? Again as both characters found self-respect and a bit of self-knowledge they gained the confidence to go for what they wanted underneath it all – a relationship with a good man. They stopped having what I call the 'I'm Unworthy Complex' and realised they were worthy of pursuing their dreams. You can too!

Great comic moments also illustrate the point about confidence, generally to great effect. Do you remember the film 'Wayne's World' where Wayne and Garth, the two main characters, were sad but lovable losers who idolised Alice Cooper? In the scene where they finally get to meet Alice they get down on their knees and start chanting, 'We're not worthy!' Of course it was an extremely funny scene that in reality played on *all* of our secret fears – that we're *not worthy* of some of the people we meet.

Too many women I come across feel this way – that somehow they're not worthy of dating the men they meet. And when you develop the 'I'm Unworthy Complex' men can see it from a million miles away! Confidence will get you your man roughly 6 times out of 10. Two out of ten men will *only* want sex – so your levels of confidence won't matter a jot to them ('They all want sex,' you might be saying at this moment but most are willing to look for your other special qualities, too!). And about two out of ten men will be the sort who wants to 'look after you' (as if you don't have a brain!) or 'control you' – so your confidence will be threatening to them.

There are two crucial effects of the 'I'm Unworthy Complex'. Either you attract those men (just mentioned) who *love* a woman to feel unworthy. This way they can take advantage of your vulnerabilities, have everything their own way, and generally behave badly to you. Or the good men aren't interested because quite simply *confidence is attractive*! A lack of it is *unattractive*. There's that message again!

Jan is a case in point of the 'I'm Unworthy Complex'. She didn't seem to lack confidence when I first met her. She was attractive, bright, and had an interesting job in television. She came to talk about her unhappiness at being single when all her friends were settling down. I asked her to run through her last few experiences of dating in micro-date-detail so I could really get a feel for her dating behaviour. It quickly became apparent that Jan was about as exciting and confident around men as a damp sponge. She quite simply became totally submissive, expecting them to take the lead in conversation, make all the choices, and do all the ringing, planning, etc. She totally relegated all her own desires and needs to last place (not even second place!) and acted as if she was 'unworthy' of even having them (I'm *not* talking sexual here!). Now when women act like this, men get very bored. They don't want a 'yes' person – they want someone with an active brain that's confident enough to use it! Because otherwise there's no chemistry – how boring!

I can assure you I promptly put Jan on a programme learning to use all my dating tactics. It only took her a few weeks to let go (as she did with girlfriends anyway) and develop the confidence to enjoy *being herself* with the men she met! And that means the Jan who knows what she wants to do, and has the confidence to flirt and have fun, as dating should be. What a happy ending to a desperate dating story.

The strange thing about the 'I'm Unworthy Complex' is that most of the women (like Jan) who've got it are actually very worthy, interesting and lovable women. They just don't know it!

ARE YOU UNWORTHY?
Let's dive straight into TACTIC THREE with a quiz!

CAUTION ALERT! It's really not going to help you develop your worthiness/confidence if you can't be honest with your answers.

1. **Do you give up *your* interests in order to pursue *his* when dating?**
A. Yes, and I've had to do some boring things like fishing when I actually hate it
B. No, I'd *never* consider giving up any interests
C. Sometimes I've tried things a date likes simply because I think it's a good thing to do

2. **When asked what you'd like to do on a date, do you –**

A. Try to guess what they want to do and suggest that?
B. Always state what you want to do?
C. Suggest a couple of options bearing in mind your tastes and what you know of his?

3. When thinking about a date's ex-girlfriends would you –
A. Always assume they're 'better' than you?
B. Not think twice about what they're like?
C. Wonder what they're like but probably wouldn't ask?

4. Would your past relationships be characterised by you as –
A. Giving, giving, giving?
B. Gimme, gimme, gimme?
C. Having some give and take?

3 or 4 As – UNWORTHY!
You've got it bad. You've probably allowed dates to walk all over you in the past, and you've probably lost out on some good men because of your lack of confidence. Pay attention to all the advice that follows in TACTIC THREE.

3 or 4 Bs – TOO WORTHY!
Wow! You may not give a guy a chance. You can be too worthy – where confidence becomes *arrogance*. Your overly worthy approach actually may be quite self-centred, and you could lose out on some good men by always insisting things go your way. You should focus on the advice throughout TACTIC THREE to find more balance in your approach to men.

3 or 4 Cs – YOU'RE WORTHY!

You probably have a good balance in being confident with dates without losing sight that both your interests are valid. You wouldn't allow a man to take advantage of you, and you wouldn't of them.

A Mixture of Answers – SITUATIONAL UNWORTHINESS!

Your worthiness depends on the situation. If you check out your answers you'll probably be able to work out where you need to build confidence. That is, what sort of situations you find daunting and then tend to behave in an unworthy way. Your reaction to a date's ex-girlfriend perhaps? Or maybe a lack of confidence to say what you'd like to do on a date?

THE TELLTALE SIGNS MEN NOTICE!

How good are men at 'sussing' out a woman with the 'I'm Unworthy Complex'? Funnily enough, they're pretty darn good at it. We always hear of women's intuition but men have intuition too. They simply appear to use it less *obviously*. But in my years of talking with people it's amazing what men have confided to me, showing how much *they can tell* about your confidence – or lack of. Here are some of the most common things men notice – the 'dirty dozen' telltale signs of 'unworthiness':

(1) A woman with shy or awkward body language. Yes, body language again! Men read body language as a barometer of confidence.
(2) A woman who won't say what she wants to do.
(3) When a woman picks at her food during a date in a restaurant – and there's nothing wrong with the food!
(4) A woman who appears desperately eager to please.

(5) When a woman feigns interest in something she's clearly not at all interested in.

(6) When a woman wants to know every detail of his relationship history.

(7) A woman who asks to be compared to an ex – e.g. 'Am I as attractive as your ex?' A huge give away!

(8) A woman who gushes about the success of her *past* love life.

(9) A woman who gushes about how many men are asking her out *right now*. No man with any confidence himself ever believes this one!

(10) Without prompting – a woman who claims she's not looking for 'anything right now'. Again, men don't buy this and read the opposite into it – that she's desperately looking for love.

(11) Overly flirtatious behaviour (more on this in TACTIC FOUR!) and too much touching. Body language again! When a woman *repeatedly* tries to 'close' the two personal spaces – this appears as desperately lonely and in need of cuddles. It's the human version of a 'wounded puppy' and definitely signals the 'I'm Unworthy Complex'!

(12) When a woman asks about his 'relationships' with his family. Men treat this as really personal info – not to be shared for a while. Again viewed as a sign of neediness that in turn is a sign of low confidence.

DATING SURVIVAL STRATEGY:
After studying the 'dirty dozen' list of telltale signs above, make a note here of how many you're guilty of:

....
....

Are there any other such 'behaviours' not on this list that you're guilty of – if so what are they?

....

....

Alternative tactic: Fill in here what the alternative 'worthy' behaviour could be (e.g. if you *never* say what you want to do, think up two ideas for ways to spend dates in future)

....

....

WHAT MAKES A WOMAN GIVE OUT THE 'I'M UNWORTHY VIBE'?

There are so many things that affect your feelings of confidence and whether or not you'll suffer the 'I'm Unworthy Complex'. Identifying what's at the root of this 'complex' is really important. Otherwise it'll hold you back from mastering TACTIC THREE – being confident!

Here are a few common reasons I've come across:

/ **Never having been encouraged to express yourself and your needs.** Many women quite simply grow up in families where the boys are allowed to express themselves, have an opinion, get out and do things – but they weren't. Old habits die hard, and so these women grow up into women who feel they can't express themselves when, e.g., dating.

♥ **Solution:** Start in situations with friends by learning how to say what you want to do, ask what you'd like to ask, and generally express your opinions. Learn what this feels like – good, hopefully! – and start applying it on dates, too.

/ **Your size – and feelings** about it. Many, many women judge their dating worthiness – and their whole self-confidence – on their weight. I don't think this is a secret. We've all had friends who moan they'll never get asked out because of their size. Or we've been there ourselves. In my most insecure days straight after my divorce in 1992 I used to worry that the size of my hips would put a man off. I felt they were too wide. But that's before I regained my self-worth post-divorce.

♥ **Solution:** Just as you can *choose* (recall the dating survival strategy 'You Have Choices' from TACTIC ONE) to focus on your size and make it into something negative, you can just as easily choose to *focus on a positive* attribute and allow that to shine through. What can shine through for you and overcome your negative focus?

....

....

✦ **Just generally not feeling 'good enough'.** Many women simply don't feel *good* about themselves in a sort of free-floating way – they can't necessarily pin it down to anything specific but it does affect them in dating. This feeling leads them to feel they have to 'please' everyone or they'll be rejected.

♥ **Solution:** Turn this thinking on its head today. Begin to realise you *will* be rejected if you try to please everyone – because you can't. Learning to assert yourself – and please yourself – will lead to confidence – and that's attractive!

✦ **Unhappy past experiences.** Many women allow unhappy experiences with dating in the past to affect *their present*. If they've been let down, or a man didn't ring when he said he would (and simply disappeared off the scene), or they've been two-timed, they choose to colour their future dating with this negative experience.

💜 **Solution:** Select some positive experiences with the opposite sex to focus on from the past. Not *every* man has let you down or played around (or have they? In that case you need to look carefully at the type of men you're choosing in TACTIC EIGHT!) – remind yourself of this. Again you can choose to embrace negativity from your past, or choose positive memories from the past – and let them colour your present with good feelings!

DATING SURVIVAL STRATEGY: HAVE YOU RECOGNISED YOURSELF?
I recognise that my feelings of being 'unworthy' in dating may come from:

....
....

My solution is:

....
....

WHAT MAKES A 'WORTHY' WOMAN?
So what magical qualities do women who feel 'worthy' have? And that men *notice* they have? You could pretty much reverse the 'dirty dozen' telltale signs of 'unworthiness' and that would be a great starting point. For example, men view as *confident* a woman who doesn't feel she has to gush about all the men who are 'after' her, and one who doesn't ask to be compared to a date's ex-girlfriend. Or how about a woman who uses simple but confident body language – like the good posture and the open smile mentioned in TACTIC TWO? Of course 'worthy', confident women aren't desperately eager to please, know what they'd like to do on a date, and *don't* hang all over his every word and his arm and thigh, too! These are very attractive, confident qualities – that you can practise!

Here are a few other points to consider in applying TACTIC THREE to dating. Confident women who *don't* suffer the 'I'm Unworthy Complex' *do* the following:

- **Seize dating opportunities!** Scenario: An interesting/cute man has stopped to chat to you. A confident woman seizes the opportunity and asks him for a coffee. Or flirts a bit. Just enough to let him know she's interested. I've never had any woman complain that she wished she'd *missed* more opportunities. But they do complain to me that they failed to seize opportunities!

- **Set goals and go for them!** A confident woman knows that she should always challenge herself (and not just with men!). But she spots someone new and attractive at a work conference and she sets a goal for getting him into a conversation. A smart woman who doesn't miss out!

- **Is not averse to creating a bit of mystery around herself!** A confident woman recognises that creating some chemistry between the sexes is a good, fun thing. She knows how to employ a little mystery to go a long way (more of that fun stuff in TACTIC NINE!).

- **Is confident enough to get what she wants out of dating!** A confident woman knows what she wants. At some points in her life she simply wants a guy to go out and have fun with – not to hear wedding bells. At other times she recognises that maybe it's the right time in terms of career, etc. to settle down – that at an emotional level that's what she wants.

- **Knows when to cut her losses!** A confident woman knows when she's flogging a dead horse. For example, she recognises quickly a man who doesn't make her feel good about herself or an unreliable man (haven't we all been there! But many of us stick with it too long!). More on this in TACTIC TEN.

DATING SURVIVAL STRATEGY: setting a confidence goal

You only need to select a few of the above – reversing the 'dirty dozen' or the other points, in order to enhance your levels of dating confidence.

List the three points above you'd most like to strive for:

....

....

Now copy these points out and post this where you'll see them!

CONFIDENCE AND THE REST OF YOUR LIFE!

Don't forget that confidence is important in all aspects of your life – work, friendships, handling family affairs, day to day living, etc. So *go forth and apply* what you've learned about dating confidence to every other aspect of your life.

The most important thing I've learned from TACTIC THREE is:

....

....

And I'm not going to forget this!

TACTIC 4:
BE ...

SEXY not easy!

We've really got ourselves in a state when it comes to dating and sex! Sure it's great we have the freedom to choose *when* to have sex, *who* to have it with, and *how* often. But why then has all this freedom left so many women feeling bad about their sexual encounters and with shattered hopes? Because there's one crucial point many women miss, and that is – *you* may want dating *and* sex *and* then perhaps a relationship (or in some other order). But *he* may simply want sex – and may not be so bothered with the rest!

  * CAUTION ALERT!* This really is true – re-read the last two sentences! It's the difference between two people's expectations that leads to heartache, embarrassment, and dreadful feelings of, 'Why *on earth* did I slip between his sheets?'

The Self-Centred Nature of Human Beings!
Why do we expect that men (or anyone for that matter!) would want the same things we do, or feel the same

way? Because as humans we are essentially self-centred. The world revolves around us! *Our* game plan may include dating, romance, a relationship and sex. But someone else's may not – it may only include sex. But we often can't get our heads around this most basic fact.

You may be thinking, 'But why don't we "suss" out what a man wants and then make decisions based on that? Women are supposed to have such intuition, aren't they?' But again, when we *really* want something – like to date and be in a romance – we see what we *want* to see! And this isn't necessarily reality. That is why TACTIC TWO (first impressions and dates) was really very important. It gave you the basic building-blocks to think about how you come across *and* the messages he's giving off. Much more of this, though, in TACTIC SEVEN – where you'll find out how to sort the princes from the frogs.

This self-centred nature, coupled with our expectations of what we want and the difficulties we face in modern dating, makes things complicated in terms of that very important, potentially intoxicating and powerful 'drug' that is sex. Sex has the power to make us soar to heights of pleasure (yes, I'm using this cliché as people feel this intensely about sex!) and intimacy with another human being. But it also has the power to lead us into dreadful decisions and behaviour *and* to be soul destroying.

That's where my TACTIC FOUR comes in – to help ensure you make it through the complicated maze of modern sex, and come out the other side getting what you want. It's up to YOU to decide what that is. I'm not here to judge anyone who says they simply want some sex and fun, but I assume you're reading THE DATING SURVIVAL GUIDE because you actually want to find romance and love, too.

MEN AND SEX

Human sexual behaviour is a complicated subject so I'm going to speak in generalisations for the next couple of sections – but *meaningful* generalisations! Ninety-nine per cent of single men will take sex when it's offered – that's true and there are few exceptions (well, maybe 90% as some may not be interested or feel up to it for one reason or another – like having drunk too much!). But they won't go on to imbue it with 'special feelings' – a rosy glow of romance and love. Let's turn to the study of psychobiology and men's genes and sex. Ancient men spread their seed far and wide when the opportunity provided itself. Sure, social groups existed that in some ways were more sophisticated than you'd think. And within these groups, couple-dom existed. However if when out hunting and gathering, a sexual opportunity presented itself, ancient men would take what they could. It was a biological imperative that drove men to try and carry on their family lines as best they could by 'sowing their wild oats'.

This behaviour is deeply rooted in a man's genes affecting modern men and their drive for sex, too. 'Yeah right, thanks Dr. Pam for giving them an excuse to go out and sow their wild oats,' you may be thinking. But I'm *not* giving men an excuse. This is not an ancient landscape! They are not hunting and gathering across woodlands and plains. They can *choose* to keep their trousers on, just as a woman can choose to keep her knickers up. However, when presented with an opportunity for sex, most single men will take it without bothering to pursue a romance with the woman.

Why not? Because the other part of a man's genetic make-up suggests that 'the chase' is very important in placing a 'value' on a sexual partner. The more desirable the partner – the higher the value. And a man will assume that a woman who'll fall into bed with him will do so with *any* man – decreasing her social value. This sounds really harsh talking about 'value' – but if I don't explain the reality to you, you may get hurt.

What did 'the chase' and 'value' mean in ancient-man terms? It meant that an ancient man, choosing a woman with 'high value' (i.e. who had to be 'chased'), would stand a better chance that the offspring he was hunting and providing for were *actually* his. And why would he want to do all that hard work for some other man's child?

I agree we've come a long way since the time of ancient men and women. However we do *not* shake off our genetic heritage so quickly. There are echoes of the past lurking in all our souls affecting our dating and relationship behaviour. Why, after women's lib, do so many women still feel driven to stay at home after the birth of a child for as *long* as possible? It's the *minority* of women who leave and go back to work, briefcase happily in hand, without feeling absolutely torn between their baby and their financial/work responsibilities. It's because our 'nurturing' role is deeply rooted in our genes. As ancient women we gave birth and were tied to the settlement while nursing our offspring, leaving the men to do the hunting and gathering – and oat-sowing!

WOMEN AND SEX

That nurturing role spreads to most of our encounters. So if we happen to have sex earlier than planned with a man, women tend to want to *nurture* a relationship out of it, or at least turn it into a 'meaningful encounter'. They don't want to let it pass as 'simply sex'. Most of us want to imbue a sexual encounter with *some* emotion. Before anyone gets on their high horse and says, 'But there are loads of liberated young women out there having as much sex as they want and that's great! Just look at all the Ibiza footage on TV!' Take on the role of agony aunt, psychologist and life coach that I've had for many years and check out how many of those women turn to you saying, 'It all feels so shallow. I feel empty after these encounters. It's not fun any more.' Then you may revise your belief that no-strings sex is good for your well-being – for most women it's not! And I actually don't believe it's good for most men either – but that's another book.

'SEX AND THE MESSAGE *YOU* GIVE' CHECKLIST

No matter what your feelings are about when it's 'right' to have sex, the message you give off is important. This checklist will open your eyes to this message and how it may or may not reflect what's *really* on your dating agenda – a bit of fun/sex or more!

Please circle the answer that fits how you mostly feel.

1.	Do you pride yourself on your sexual prowess, skills and/or techniques?	YES/NO
2.	Do you dress to *thrill* for first dates?	YES/NO
3.	Do you feel cheated if you don't get a passionate kiss at the end of a first date?	YES/NO
4.	Could you 'flirt for Britain'?	YES/NO
5.	Do a man's looks mean more to you than anything else?	YES/NO
6.	Has a man ever suggested you were over-sexed/too flirty?	YES/NO
7.	Do you expect a man to 'come on' to you during the first date?	YES/NO
8.	Do you find it hard to say 'No' to sex with a date?	YES/NO
9.	Do you make sexy jokes with a new date?	YES/NO
10.	Have you ever regretted any sexual encounters?	YES/NO

SEX & YOU KEY:
5 to 10 YES answers: Sex Bomb!

Watch out if you want *more* than sex from a man. They may read you as being a bit of a sex bomb or worse yet – 'easy'! If you're practising safer sex, have rock-hard confidence, and only want sex, this is fine. Otherwise if you're using sex, or an over-sexed message, to try to get *love* you're going to fall on your face – or flat on your back – if you'll pardon the pun! Follow all the TACTIC FOUR advice to get what you want.

2 to 4 YES answers: Flirt!

You can be fairly flirty but that's fine as long as you're not being a good old-fashioned 'tease' (see below). Also be aware if your YES answers include no. 8 or 10 – you may be vulnerable to risky decisions you then feel bad about. YES answers to no. 1 or 6 could also lead you into some dodgy behaviour. So think about your YES answers, the message they give, and follow the advice in TACTIC FOUR.

0 to 1 YES answers: Innocent!

You're probably in control of your sexual behaviour and the message you give out, but on the other hand you may also be shy about being sexy. If your NO answers reflect a fear of flirting then again you should take notice of recommendations in TACTIC FOUR to get your message just right.

BEING SEXY AND HAVING SEX ARE TWO VERY DIFFERENT THINGS!

One problem that many women face is to grasp the concept that they can be very sexy without having sex. *There is no rule* that states if you have a certain sexiness about you – or sex appeal – then you have to *have* sex. It's being *confident* in yourself combined with sex appeal that means you can have the best of both worlds – your date sits up and takes notice of you, but you won't have sex until *you're* ready.

What makes a woman sexy?

Now to help you along with your sexual confidence let's delve into the recesses of the male mind (Do we *really* want to go there?). Having spoken to hundreds (thousands even!) of men in my agony aunt career in particular, I've distilled a list of things *they* say are sexy. This is not an exhaustive list but easily applicable.

CAUTION ALERT! Each individual man will emphasise different points on this list as being sexy:

- A woman who can have a good laugh. Really throwing back her head and letting go is very sexy. Tittering quietly is homely!
- A *warm* woman – bitchiness is off the sexy-menu. So don't make bitchy remarks about people and things until you've been dating a while.
- A woman who dresses for the occasion and then *forgets* about her looks! Yes, peeking in each mirror as you walk into a restaurant is a big turn-off for men. Sure *they* can mirror-gaze but they don't want their date to!
- A woman with an appetite. This has come up in TACTIC TWO – First Impressions. There's nothing sexy about a woman who orders food and then picks at it. A man's subconscious mind tells him that a hungry woman will also be 'hungry' in bed!
- A woman who'll at least show a *little* interest in his man-hobbies. You don't have to pretend to be football-mad but making sweeping generalisations about how boring the game is, is a turn-off. Don't ask me how they link this into sexiness but they do!

- Revealing clothes in small doses are sexy. Again, men find a revealing top *or* skirt sexy. But both together say 'easy'. You may ask why they drool over really skimpily dressed models in magazines but don't necessarily want a date to wear so little – because the model is a fantasy figure. You are their reality and even if men don't admit it most are looking at you as potential partner material.
- Fun flirting is sexy, but in-your-face remarks about sex are not. But more on flirting further on.
- Compliments are sexy. Yes, men have egos too and love it when you say something like, 'I love your hair cut,' or shirt, or whatever!
- Soft vocal tones are sexy – loud boisterous tones are manly – and they don't want to date a man! That said, some men find very assertive women sexy. But I'll leave you to judge if your date is one of these.
- A woman who has something to say about her life is sexy! This goes back to TACTIC THREE – your dating confidence. If you say nothing about your life, desires, and ambitions, he'll think you do nothing with it – not interesting so not sexy!

DATING SURVIVAL STRATEGY:
How many of the above can you honestly claim to do?

....
....

Which two could you easily add to your dating arsenal? (e.g. I could say more about my life on a date.)

....
....

What message does the list above tell you about men and sex? It tells me:

....

....

The following is what it *tells me* – check out how similar it is to your answer. It tells *me* that men don't find 'extremes' sexy – extreme clothing, extreme flirting, extreme behaviours (e.g. bitchy behaviour, loudness). Men find confidence, individuality, and pretty much *comforting* behaviour sexy, e.g. speaking up for yourself (so they know what you'd like to eat, do, think), soft voice (hmmm, this might remind them of their mums cooing over them when they were little!), and humour (laughing at their jokes is comforting to their ego after all!).

COMMON QUESTIONS (AND THE ANSWERS) ABOUT SEX!

Women frequently ask me the following questions, which will give *you* food for thought.

If I put sex on a platter what's saying we won't have such great sex that he wants a relationship too?

This old myth that you can ensnare a man with such great sex that he'll want a relationship only rarely pans out! If you put it on a platter you're far more likely to become a feast that he visits only *when hungry*. Sure, some relationships start with great sex as a basis but again based on my experience talking to vast numbers of people, this is a rarity.

Do men 'test' women by exerting sexual pressure to see their reaction?

Yes, men do exert sexual pressure for this reason and others. They 'try it on' to see if you'll go to bed with them. If you succumb many will judge your social value as low. Sadly men have a double standard and still slap friends on the back for their conquests. But they want to have a relationship with someone who's not a pushover because when you finally go to bed with them, it makes *them feel special* if you've made them wait.

CAUTION ALERT! – If he keeps pressuring you and won't believe it when you say 'No' – dump him. He has no respect for anything except what's going on in his trousers. Some men are complete 'chancers' and this excessive pressure is one sign. Don't fall for it! I define excessive pressure as something that's too much in *your book* – use your intuition!

How can I tell if it's lust or love?

The 'chemistry' phase of a relationship consists of our hormones conspiring to drive us mad! You two fancy each other like crazy but you don't want to have low 'value' so you keep him waiting. Things get so *intense* you start to feel it *must* be love. Then you risk fooling yourself into going to bed thinking it's got to be the real thing. If you're *unlucky* your fledgling relationship ends after having sex. Lust can develop into love but only with time and care. When it's *pure lust* you two spend all your time 'frustrating' each other – you know what I mean – snogging and fondling each other but stopping short of having sex. Not going out to do things together, but spending all your time rolling about on the sofa! If you find you *only* think about the physical side with him, you don't have that much to say to each other, if you can't keep your hands off each other and you keep taking it to the edge – it's lust. If you two are doing *other things* – like going out on proper dates and keeping your hands to yourself at least occasionally, then it's got a chance to develop into something more.

What's the big deal – why is my body so precious?

How can we have come to this state when I get asked this question? Liberation is great but part of that is knowing *what* to cherish in your life! Do you really want to give away the most intimate part of you – your own body – to someone who may only see it as 'dessert' after a date? To someone who won't cherish it? The big deal is that your body should be precious to you – it's not there to have sweaty, uncaring, over-sexed hands creep around it! Now if that thought doesn't put women off too-early sex I don't know what will! Most of us make mistakes when it comes to having sex. But you have the chance NOW to make decisions you'll feel good about, that'll get you the romance and relationship you want. You simply need to absorb this advice based on so much information and experience (no I *haven't* had that much personal experience – I'm talking about professional experience of hearing people's stories and knowing about human nature!).

What if he doesn't want to keep seeing me if I won't sleep with him?

Then he's not worth seeing! It's as simple as that. If a man says you have to have sex to go out with him he's a selfish, disrespectful, and unworthy person. As well as being an emotional blackmailer – because blackmail it is! No matter how much you've fooled yourself into thinking he's gorgeous and you desperately want to be the one who 'captures' him – he's not going to treat you well, that's for sure.

Can men separate sex from emotion?

Some sensitive men *can't* separate sex and emotion. They have a much more 'feminine' attitude that sex should be special and emotionally charged. That said, some of the *newest* of 'new' men I've met can still be heard joking with 'the lads' about 'giving her one'.

I've slept with men quickly before so does it matter now?

Yes, it matters now! The next man may be 'the one' so why risk things with him? Each relationship is different so allow yourself to behave differently this time.

I really like him and hope it goes past the first few dates – how do I handle the sex-thing?

This common *and* important question brings me to the 'right time for sex'. This deserves its own section which now follows!

THE RIGHT TIME FOR SEX

I'm going to keep my answer simple. The reason being is that when you're awash with the excitement of a new date, and flushed with love hormones (don't they feel *great*? But they're so dangerous!) only the clearest message will get through to you! The 'right time' consists of two main elements:

1. Communication: You two need to be able to *talk* about important things before you have sex. You need to be able to listen to the other, and understand the other. These points make for good communication. Why? you might ask. Because if you've got to the point where you can talk about the 'meaning of life', your hopes and dreams, and can be honest with each other – then you've got a decent basis for having sex. If you *can't talk* then you don't know what he really wants. If you can't talk to him about what his expectations are for your dating and/or budding romance then you really shouldn't sleep with him – if you're interested in more than sex, that is. And also how will you be able to have good sex? Good sex after all is about communication of your needs to the other. If again, he can't understand your need to develop good communication then he's unlikely to be good romance material.

2. Confidence: You need to have the confidence in yourself to believe your intuition about him, his motives and his expectations. In other words you shouldn't be in a state of doubt about what his intentions are where you're concerned. You also need to have the confidence that once you go to bed with him, *if* it all goes wrong (i.e. the relationship doesn't last), you won't be devastated that you had sex *too quickly*. Because if there's a doubt about whether it's still too soon, then *it is too soon*! You can never have control when things take a negative turn – e.g. he gets cold feet or decides you're not right for him (or you get cold feet!). But you can insure against a negative turn by *knowing* what your reasons are for having sex. And the confidence that these are the right reasons. If it's to keep hold of him – No, that's not a good reason! If your confidence about him and you is high, and the time feels right – Yes, that's the right reason!

Having made these two points, no couple (or fledgling couple) will reach these points at the same pace or in the same way, which is why I can't say something really simple like there's a 'three week' or 'three month' rule for the right time for sex.

FLIRTING WILL GET YOU EVERYWHERE

While you're waiting to decide about the sex-thing you can have loads of fun flirting. Flirting is a great thing. It quite simply smooths the path of communication and puts a spring in your step. Flirting also gives out the message that you're interested – but it doesn't give the game away by saying exactly *how* interested! So it'll keep him on his toes. Follow my simple 'guide' to flirt your way to fun and romance.

Dos and don'ts of flirting

 We've already discussed some flirting behaviours in TACTIC TWO – maybe you should look at that section again.

 Flirting versus teasing. Flirting involves subtle signs of *interest*. Teasing involves signals that promise '*action*' and then the person doesn't deliver. Think about this difference!

💜 Giving knowing looks is a great starting point. Your look should say, 'I find *you* attractive!'

💜 The glint in your eye. They say the eyes are the windows to the soul so allowing them to linger on his is very flirty. The message is that you want to let him into your thoughts – a bit!

💜 Compliments – I've mentioned these earlier. Men enjoy them and it's a perfect way to flirt. Tell him he smells good if you like his aftershave. Say he's got great taste or you love his jokes (all men love this!).

💜 Be flirty with the things you say. A great way to flirt is to turn questions around with a mischievous smile. If for example he asks when you last went out with someone ask him why *he's so interested*!

💜 When he rings keep the conversation *short and fun* so you keep him wanting more.

💜 Get playful – if you two are having a goodnight kiss tickle him a little or break it off and say, 'Down boy!' Being playful can keep things from getting too heavy and men love a bit of larking about. It keeps their minds off any 'emotional' developments that are percolating in their subconscious.

💜 When he asks you out pretend to be busy for two weeks. As his face drops tell him you were kidding and that you're free, e.g., two days later.
When you know him a bit more you can comment on his *sexy* dancing (yes, some men are good dancers!) or *sexy* kisses. In other words you can be more forward with your choice of words.

💜 Double entendres. This means 'double meaning' in French. Occasionally you can emphasise something you say with a glint in your eye giving it a double meaning. It's very 'Carry On' but that's fun and flirty!

♥ Serious flirting should be saved for when your dating is getting more serious. This involves a bit of *teasing* so you have to know the territory, i.e. the man! Will he take it in the spirit it's intended (fun!) or read more into it than you mean? This flirting involves whispering how much you love his cute bottom when you two are cuddling, or you mess around to the point of 'no return' saying you know the wait will be worth it!

Now you can put TACTIC FOUR to work for you! You know he'll *take* sex if you *offer* it. You now know most men *still* have a double standard and judge your social 'value' by how quickly you go to bed, no matter how harsh that sounds. But more importantly I want *you* to value your self-esteem by valuing your body. I want you to be in *control* when you choose to have sex. And to have the confidence to know when that time is right – that he won't dump you if a relationship is what you're after! Sex is a fantastic thing – I've written many articles about it, but my underlying message is that sex is definitely at its best when there's feelings involved on *both* sides – love, trust and caring. That means waiting longer so that those men who are slow to acknowledge their feelings have time to catch up with yours.

The most important thing I've learned from TACTIC FOUR is:

....

....

And I'm not going to forget this!

TACTIC 5:
BE ...

BUSY – avoid the 'Princess Syndrome'!

Crack open some chilled white wine, sit back and sip it slowly while you absorb this TACTIC. A lot of women fall down on this one! The trap they fall into (I've even been guilty of this in the past!) I've labelled 'The Princess Syndrome'. 'What on earth is that?' you're wondering right now. Think back to the Age of Chivalry when knights jousted on horseback, kingdoms were won and lost in raging battles, and the hands of fair maidens were highly sought. Princesses sat in castle windows hoping their favourite knight would pass by and look up at them (think Romeo and Juliet to get a good visual image). You may think this *sounds* very romantic but what if your favourite prince failed to ride past? You'd be stuck up that tower feeling very lonely and bored! Probably wondering what was the matter with *you*, *as well*.

With the very rare exception (e.g. Queen Elizabeth I) women had a very passive role in times gone by. In fact it was downright unwomanly for them to make any moves in the game of romance. Instead they had to play a waiting game. And it could be a long one with knights going off on crusades, conquering distant lands, and bringing home riches to their kings. 'But stop, why look at history,' you may be saying, '*we* don't have to wait around anymore!' That's so true. But women still *do* wait around for the phone to ring, for him to pop by, or hoping he'll show up in the pub in which they first set eyes on each other. And that's why I've labelled it 'The Princess Syndrome', because this waiting behaviour harks back to a distant time when it was considered the right way to behave. We don't have to do that any more but trust me, nine out of ten women have been caught up in this syndrome at some point.

ARE YOU A POTENTIAL PRINCESS IN WAITING?
Complete the following checklist to see how vulnerable you are to 'The Princess Syndrome':

1. Have you ever checked your phone to see if it's faulty or come unplugged? YES/NO
2. Have you ever missed an evening out with friends in the hope that 'Mr. P.' would ring? YES/NO
3. Have you ever hung around a place you know 'Mr. P.' does in the hopes of 'accidentally' bumping into him? YES/NO
4. Have you ever tried to get to know a man's friends so that you could get more access to him? YES/NO
5. Have you ever told a friend you can't be on the phone long as you're waiting for 'Mr. P.' to ring? YES/NO
6. Do you believe in love at first sight as opposed to it being lust? YES/NO
7. Have you actually *changed* other plans to accept a date with 'Mr. P.'? YES/NO

8. Do you hold out to the last minute hoping for an invitation from a possible date before accepting another? YES/NO

9. Do you use a 'different' voice (more girly?) when answering the phone if you think it's 'Mr. P.'? YES/NO

10. Have you ever called him, withholding your phone number, to see if he's in (and not calling you!)? YES/NO

'THE PRINCESS SYNDROME' KEY:
1 or 2 YES answers: Acceptable levels of 'The Princess Syndrome'!

All of us have waited by the phone on occasions. If someone's particularly special and they have said they'd ring on 'Tuesday night' then it seems quite natural. *Unless* you keep checking to see if the phone's functioning (that's obsessive!). Or you withhold your number and ring to see if he's in – and hasn't called yet (that's stalking behaviour!). So examine the one or two items you've said 'YES' to and decide whether they were 'princess-y' or legitimate.

3 to 5 YES answers: Not quite a 'Princess' but a Lady in Waiting!

You've got it pretty bad but at times you probably manage to control your 'princess' impulses. Have you answered YES to nos. 2, 3, 4, 7, 8 or 10? These are particularly negative behaviours and would constitute a full-blown 'Princess Syndrome'. Read and follow the coming advice.

6 to 10 YES answers: Fully blown 'Princess Syndrome'!

There are no two ways about it – you've got 'The Princess Syndrome'! You probably already know this as friends and family have commented on your phone 'obsessions' and that you've got to 'get out more and stop waiting for his call!' You've probably done this over and over with various men you've waited for, but if you want dating success you definitely need to take all the advice of TACTIC FIVE on board – so turn your phone off now and get stuck in.

Jenny was a complete 'princess' when I met her. She'd lost friends over waiting by the phone for men to call. She'd been caught out skulking around the hangout of the last man she'd fancied and he'd never rung her after that. Jenny had even replaced a few phones, convinced that they had 'intermittent' faults. Oh yes, they worked whenever a friend, family member or cold-caller rang, but not when a 'Mr. P.' was on the horizon.

It was her mum who convinced her she needed some confidence boosting and she came to me for 'life coaching'.

What we had to work on most – besides building her basic confidence – was Jenny's irrational belief that if you weren't there to take a call, a man wouldn't call back again. With some 'challenging' and role-play, Jenny came to find that she was most interested when a man was a 'bit of a challenge' *himself*. She now needed to be a bit of a challenge back – and being 'on tap' at the end of the phone was not challenging!

It took a while for Jenny to break her bad dating habits, but once she realised that they were habits to be broken – and she did it – she was much happier. Last word Jenny was happily dating a 'Mr. P.' for three months without any panics over the phone.

WHY MEN DON'T WANT A PRINCESS!

You may think it's quite romantic being a bit of a princess. The *pain and doubt* you go through as you wait by that phone; the *flutters* of excitement in your stomach when the phone rings; and the *depths* of despair when it's someone cold-calling to flog you life insurance! In actual fact this isn't real romance, it's a bit of torture for your already low self-esteem. Yes, if you've got 'The P.S.' you've probably got low self-esteem, and as strongly noted in TACTIC THREE confidence and self-esteem are valued by *worthy* men. *What* would actually happen if you didn't wait by that phone or *semi-stalk* his hangouts?

A 'PRINCESS' THINKS:

- 'Mr. P.' will never ring back (unlikely!)
- He'll think you're too busy and not interested (unlikely again!)
- He'll ring someone else from his little black book (so he's Mr. Popular is he? Unlikely again!)
- There'll never be anyone else (well how silly is that?)
- You're not missing anything anyway by staying by the phone (how much would your friends like that?)

A WOMAN WITH DATING SUCCESS *POTENTIAL* KNOWS:

- He will ring back!
- If he can't be bothered to ring back then he wasn't very interested – and he wouldn't have been a very attentive date!
- There will always be another man (high confidence!)
- It's going to be fun going out with friends!
- She doesn't have the time to sit by the phone!
- She couldn't imagine skulking around his haunts!

DATING SURVIVAL STRATEGY:

Can you see the difference between the two lists? I hope so!

Write down your worst fear if you happen to miss his phone call: (e.g. He'd never call again)

....

....

Write out a replacement slogan with a 'fighting' spirit: (e.g. 'If he can't be bothered to ring again I can't be bothered to wait!')

....

....

Write out the three best reasons why he should fall for you and ring you back:

....

....

It's High Maintenance –

There are other reasons why men don't find a 'princess' romantic. Princesses by their very definition are going to be high maintenance, and most men don't want high maintenance! Some maintenance of course, to kick-start a fledgling romance, but high maintenance – scary! The kind of high maintenance I'm talking about is constant reassurance. Because if they have rung you (and of course being a 'princess' you were there to take their call) it doesn't stop there. If you've got such low self-esteem that you give up everything waiting for his call, then you're going to need various types of reassurance down the line.

For example, he'll need to reassure you, if he mentions his 'ex', that he's NOT carrying a torch for her. If he mentions his mum, you'll worry he's a 'mummy's boy' and you'll be in competition with *her*! If he talks about work, you'll think he should be focusing more on you. If he focuses the conversation on you, you'll think he's trying to 'suss' you out as potential mate-material, and *worry* he'll discover your lack of confidence. And so it goes on. Those behaviours are high maintenance and men soon tire of them. The insecure 'princess' loses out!

It's Boring –

You may think a man would love to have you *on tap* down the end of the phone. But you're neglecting their very nature and the thrill of the chase (unless he's as needy as you are and then you can both go cocoon yourselves from life!). This was covered thoroughly in TACTIC FOUR. A man would like to think you *have a life* other than him ringing you. It'll seem slightly odd to him if you're always in. A man's mind will go to that dark place and wonder, 'Doesn't she have any friends? What's wrong with her?' He may even wonder why there are no potential love rivals on the scene. Now that *would* make you exciting and more of a challenge.

Get a Life Not a Castle Window – Strategies to Prevent 'The Princess Syndrome'!

You can put the following into practice immediately – or when you meet the next man you're interested in.

★ Break a habit for life and force yourself NOT to answer the phone one evening per week – to anyone.

★ Make sure you have a fun but not OTT message on your answering machine. If it's user-friendly he'll be more likely to leave a message (which you want). If it's OTT or totally mad, etc., he may be a bit intimidated. Men are such tender creatures!

★ Use a friend as a crisis buddy to stop you running out and buying a new phone or checking that yours works. If you're tempted, ring her (that'll prove it's working anyway) and tell her you're going through a bad patch. Talk yourself up with her help. Friends can be great at saying things like, 'You've got so much to offer so don't worry if he hasn't rung.'

 Get out and do things, particularly when you've met a 'Mr. P.' You'll definitely arouse his interest if you have 'plans' and things to talk about.

 When you take his calls as noted in TACTIC FOUR don't stay on the line longer than ten minutes as you've got other things to do! Shorter than that actually might put his nose out of joint, but longer than that suggests you're there for his bidding.

 Make the 'other things' you've got to do *interesting.* Don't tell him you're going to do your weekly facemask or touch up your roots – ever! Well, when you two are totally in love you can be more honest about how your precious time is spent. Facemasks and root-jobs are important!

 If he rings within 12 hours of you giving him your number don't take his call. Let him leave a message. If it takes him two days – and you're in – take his call but pretend you were just on your way out! These time frames are critical. If he rings within 12 hours he's pretty keen and you can keep him waiting a little by having him leave a message. If he takes two days to ring then he may be playing the 'two day challenge' – i.e. making himself seem busy! So keep it short and make him feel lucky to have got you. If he waits three days he's pushing his luck. Either he's very busy (query workaholic); not that interested (then 'so what, his loss' – only a *non*-princess would say that – and you're becoming her!); a real 'player' (watch out); or very shy and it's taken him that long to muster the courage to ring (hard work). Use your intuition to decide!

 If he rings expecting you to be free the next day –

think twice. This means the following: a. he thinks you're not busy (read this as 'she doesn't have a life!') and maybe that you're a pushover; b. he's thoughtless or simply wasn't thinking you may have other plans; or c. he thinks you should drop things for him. I always think the date should come a couple of days after the call – this builds anticipation and gives you the chance to prepare for great first impressions (remember those?). But there are exceptions to this – again I think you should use your intuition – just be aware of how it looks if you eagerly accept a date for the next night!

★ Having a busy life is good for you! The more of 'a life' you have, the less dependent you'll be on 'Mr. P.' to provide one for you – the healthier your potential romance!

CAUTION ALERT! In your little heart you may think it's romantic depending on him – dependent love is not healthy love! Sure if you get serious with him you both may end up 'depending' on each other, but hopefully in a supportive not *needy* way.

The most important thing I've learned from TACTIC FIVE is:

....

....

And I'm not going to forget this!

TACTIC 6:
BE ...

KNOWING
not a know-it-all!

I'm sorry but the myth of men loving a 'dumb' blonde (or any other 'dumb' woman) has got to be destroyed once and for all! It's the rare man who actually wants to date someone 'dumb', or shall I be PC and say 'intellectually challenged'? Or at least more intellectually challenged than himself because, let's face it, if he's not the brightest spark he won't expect you to be either! Now how do we spend most of our first few dates with a man? *In conversation*! Over a drink, lunch, or dinner. And it's how we come across in conversation – what we know, don't know and *how* we know it – that can make or break a man's interest. He won't be interested if you know *nothing*. And let's be completely honest – the conversation in the first few days and weeks of dating is really one great façade for what you're really thinking about each other. And what you'd *really* like to say! But of course we can't say what we're really thinking when we first date – that would give the game away!

Conversation is a TACTIC to be used wisely. We've

talked about 'topical' dos and don'ts in TACTIC TWO but this is the *subtle* stuff! There's a line between being bright and knowing about things, and being a *know-it-all*. Here a man's ego enters the equation – and their egos are like delicate flowers when you're first dating! Men like to feel they can have a conversation with an *intelligent* woman, but they don't want to be *threatened* by it. They want to date an *interesting* woman, but not one interested in *scoring points* over them. So how on earth do we meet these two needs without going overboard in one direction or the other – not bright enough or knowing it all?

The answer to this reminds me of an experience I once had. I was very young (18) and dating a young barrister (22). Whenever we had a 'discussion' (read 'argument' here!) he would launch into a 'debate' as if we were in court. He'd try to lead our discussion down a logical path, scoring points along the way. It was as if I ceased to be his girlfriend and instead became his adversary. I absolutely hated that know-it-all attitude and really despaired if a subject loomed where we might disagree.

Needless to say we broke up but it gave me a personal perspective on how unpleasant it was to be on the receiving end of this style of *knowing everything* (I might add besides this he was actually a great guy!). Now from a professional perspective I've found that men hate being on the receiving end of a woman with this attitude and conversational style *even more*, because they feel their *masculinity* is threatened – and that is a very big deal! Whereas like other women who've been on the receiving end of a male know-it-all, I didn't feel my femininity was threatened. Instead I simply felt it wasn't a 'human' way of discussing a point. It was too *mechanical* as other women I've worked with have suggested.

But finding a *balance* with this issue is a particular problem as women now are go-for-it people and know how to assert themselves, which is as it should be! And this is great, of course, in the workplace, or in negotiating a house sale or purchasing a car. But it's not necessarily so great in dating and romance! Don't get me wrong, I'm not saying women shouldn't assert themselves in conversations, but it's *how* we do it that dictates our success in the game of romance!

Romantic Compromise

This is where romantic compromise is important. Sometimes the whole issue of asserting yourself and standing up for your rights gets taken too far (by *both* men and women). We forget it's not just a 'me, me, me' society but that when it comes to dating and love it should be 'we, we, we'! There are two of you to consider! If you like him enough on first meeting that you're thinking he's a 'Mr. P.' then you need to take on board TACTIC SIX in a serious way.

Equally you may be extremely shy and anxious having never asserted yourself in any area of life. But then you are liable to run into the opposite problem – of being so worried about saying the *right thing* that you come across as knowing nothing! If this is the case, taking on board TACTIC FOUR and the advice on being confident will have helped (I hope! I *am* an optimist after all!).

How to find romantic compromise!

Now without jeopardising your self-awareness and confidence there are strategies to use that'll help you find the balance between being bright and interesting, and *knowing* it all. But first I'd like you to take the following quiz to gauge how easy it'll be for you to find a conversational balance. We may not give them credit but men *do* listen to what we say and take note of our conversational style.

KNOW-IT-ALL QUIZ:
Select the answer you'd be most likely to do:

1. Do you always have to win an argument (with anyone – friend, family, colleague, etc.)? YES/NO
2. Is it more important to you to 'save face' than to be honest about something? YES/NO
3. Has anyone called you 'bossy', or a 'know-it-all' even? YES/NO
4. Do you ever 'speak before you think'? YES/NO
5. Are you in a career where asserting yourself is very important, e.g. sales or law? YES/NO
6. At school/college, or now, did you enjoy 'competitive' activities – e.g. joining sports or the debate team? YES/NO
7. Do you get easily frustrated if someone seems to know less than you about a subject? YES/NO
8. Do you find it hard to say 'sorry' or admit you're in the wrong? YES/NO
9. Have you ever dumped a man because he was more handsome than smart? YES/NO
10. Are you what people would call a 'high achiever'? YES/NO

KNOW-IT-ALL QUIZ KEY:
Up to Four YES answers: KNOWING!
As I've said before we're all fairly self-centred as human beings. So unless you're incredibly shy and unassertive you'll probably have answered 'YES' to a few of these questions. So I'm not going to penalise you for that! You're probably a 'knowing' person which is great – you can find balance in your conversations with men. What I would recommend is that if you answered 'YES' to

numbers 1, 3, 4, or 8 you should pay particular attention to the TACTIC SIX advice that follows.

Five or more YES answers: KNOW-IT-ALL!

You *are* at risk of being too much of a know-it-all where the first few dates are concerned. I wonder if you've ever put a man's nose out of joint? Did you ever think a date was going well only for him never to ring you again? Think about the conversation – were you perhaps *too* knowing – and so, too challenging? You're going to have to rein in your stronger impulses in this regard. But let's get to the main advice!

The 'know-it-all' versus 'knowing' way of being!

There are two main points to this – (1) *what* you say and (2) *how* you say it! *The following should be thought about and acted upon so you don't sound like a 'know-it all'*:

- **The Bull Dog Phenomenon!** When you get on a topic and can't let go – like a dog with a bone you hang in for the last word. Because many women feel they're competing in all areas of life, it's easy to do this on a date too. You shouldn't be in competition for the 'last word' with a man you're just getting to know.
- **Women's Intuition!** When you say you know something because 'your intuition tells you so' men get a bit wary thinking you assume they haven't got any. If you slip up and mention your intuition, throw in the fact that you wonder what his 'intuition' tells him about the topic you're discussing.
- **Broken Record!** Repeating yourself (something a research study once found that women do far more than men – oops!) comes across as if you

don't think he's got your point the first time around. So say something once and if you have to say it again, think of another way to put it!

/ **For Women Only!** Getting on to female-type topics like Hollywood gossip, what your best friend's boyfriend is like, what your best friend's recent 'diet torture/success' was like, etc. (and no I'm not sexist but certain topics are largely talked about by women) while he flails around looking for something to add makes him feel as if you're a know-it-all.

/ **Verbally Slapping Him Down!** Telling a man he's 'silly' or 'doesn't understand' is like a physical slap across the face. And when you think about it, it sounds like you're taking on a mother-role towards him – not very sexy!

/ **A Gentle Game of Tennis!** A great conversation is like a good game of tennis which neither of you should dominate. So particularly if he's shy – and loads of men hide shyness behind a bit of bravado – then serve the ball gently to him.

/ **There's Always Something You Don't Know!** Even if you know a topic inside and out, always think of one aspect you don't really know and ask him about it. It's flattering for him to think that you two can tackle a topic together.

/ **Famous Last Words!** Never say anything like, 'Oh you wouldn't understand, you're a man!' if he asks you to explain something he didn't quite get. Two things – it sounds like he's not worth you trying to put it in different words; and that you're fairly man-negative!

/ **Variety is the Spice of Life!** Bringing up lots of different topics shows off the breadth of your interests, and, more likely than not, he'll have something to say about one of them.

/ **Ask Him!** Asking him what he knows about x, y, or z, suggests you value his opinion. It's like you want to compare notes. This is flattering without you having to look less bright than you are.

/ **If Sparks Fly!** If you two happen to hit on a topic that makes you both see red towards each other, and you like him, then lay it to rest. You can graciously say something like, 'We both have something to say on this subject but why don't we talk about x, y, or z instead?' It'll demonstrate to him that you're bright and have opinions but you're also interested in a pleasant time – not a debate! Remember this is not about scoring points – he's your date not your enemy!

/ **Vocal Tone!** Yes, it's true no matter what you have to say (even if delivering a 'speech' about your pet interest that you do know everything about!) he'll listen more readily and be more accepting of what you say if you use soft, warm tones. A scolding tone like a headmistress will get you nowhere fast (unless he has a fetish for dominatrix types – who knows? Could be fun!).

/ **Temper What You Say *At First*!** You can boss him around in a know-it-all tone when you've moved in together! Just kidding – had you going there a minute didn't I!

The most important thing I've learned from TACTIC SIX is:

....

....

And I'm not going to forget this!

TACTIC 7:
BE ...

ABLE to sort the
princes from frogs!

News flash! The Office of National Statistics has found that there are now *more* 'Mr. Singletons' living on their own than at any other time in history! Single men now represent more than one in ten of homes in Britain – which is three times more than 30 years ago. So you could knock on every tenth door in your road and a 'Mr. P.' would answer it. That's not bad odds is it? But no, I don't want to suggest that you start charging out borrowing cups of sugar from the entire road just to sort out where the singles live. Another statistic is that, on average, these days men don't tend to settle down before the age of 30, compared to the 1960s when 25 was the norm.

This all sounds like good news, huh? A wealth of single men out there – ready for the picking? And, hey, if they're settling down at a later age this may mean they're more mature, understanding and ready for a relationship. Well, I don't want to dampen your hopes but this doesn't mean they're all 'Mr. P.s'! Remember a lot of these singles are single *for a reason* – they're not princes, they're frogs unworthy of your love! That brings me to the issue at the root of TACTIC SEVEN – just how do you sort the frogs from the princes?

First let's find out just how good your 'frog-radar' already is (or isn't!) with a mini-quiz.

THE FROG OR PRINCE? QUIZLET!
Choose the answer you *most* agree with. Go through the items quickly without stopping and thinking – I want your gut reactions!

1. **A man who waits five days to call is:**
A. Playing 'hard to get'
B. Not really interested

2. **A man who eyes up women as they come into a room is:**
A. A normal, hot-blooded male
B. A womaniser

3. **A man who gives you loads of compliments on the first couple of dates is:**
A. Attentive
B. Trying to get into your knickers

4. **A man who dodges questions about his past is:**
A. Shy and/or reserved
B. Secretive

5. **A man who claims you're driving him 'crazy with passion and he can't help himself' is:**
A. Truly passionate
B. After sex without commitment

The more 'A' answers you have the less likely your 'frog-radar' is working. The 'A' answers were selected to reflect naivety and an over-abundance of wanting to see the 'best in a man'. The more 'B' answers you selected the more active your 'frog-radar' is. Let's run through the questions: remember the two-day phone call rule – if he's interested he'll ring you within that time. Any longer (e.g. five days) means you're his last option. All men notice good-looking women (and all women notice good-looking men) but they should always be discreet about eyeing them up. A compliment or two is great – more than that and it's simply *not genuine*. I *know this* having interviewed thousands in my work as an agony aunt and psychologist – they simply don't give out loads of compliments at first. And even later on! If you've got onto the subject of your 'past history' then he should at least say a little. And finally men *can* control their sexual impulses – don't believe that kind of line!

How You Can Improve Your Ability to Sort the Princes From the Frogs!

The first thing to realise is that there are *different* types of frogs. I'm going to outline for you the worst, and probably the most obvious, 'offenders' and typical behaviour they're guilty of. Now when you meet someone new if these sorts of behaviours start falling into place and triggering a sense of déjà vu – be warned – your 'frog radar' is developing power! I'll also move on to more general principles to help you fully apply TACTIC SEVEN.

MUMMY'S BOY – The apron strings may be invisible but don't be fooled!

Signs to watch for:

The frog-like behaviour of a 'Mummy's Boy':

/ He rings his mother a lot.

/ He'll be late to meet you when he's been with her.

/ He'll pick at things you do that aren't the way his mum does – e.g. the way you cook or arrange your furniture, etc.

/ He won't be very physically affectionate – that's reserved for dear old mum!

/ He's also not very sexual once you get *serious*. Serious in his mind does not equate with sexiness.

/ He'll wear clothes that she's chosen – and are NOT very fashionable.

/ When ill he'll make even more of a big deal of it than the average man. And sulk if you don't fuss over him as much as 'mum' does.

The things a 'Mummy's Boy' is most likely to say:

👄 'My mother always says . . .'

👄 'You remind me of my mother . . .' – within the first few weeks this is definitely dodgy! He shouldn't be relating you *to* his mother – yet! Later on down the line you may both laugh about how you *do* remind him of his mum.

👄 When talking about making a life change or a major purchase, 'I think I should check this out with someone whose judgement I trust.' He means his mum's opinion!

👄 'You'd get on so well with my mum!' He means he's desperately hoping you will.

👄 'Family is really important.' He's probably referring to his mum.

👄 'You should do that like this . . .' as he proceeds to show you how his mother does something.

The reasons he's a frog:
You may be an optimist that you can *lure* him away from mum – don't be fooled! His mother will always come first and come between you. Not only that but his mother will be in on the act – she'll manipulate him for all she's worth! And make your life hell.

MR. SAD & NEEDY – He's the anorak-wearing, no-hoper in the game of romance who'll be thankful to have any girlfriend!
Signs to watch for:

The frog-like behaviour of a 'Mr. Sad & Needy':
- He'll do anything to please you. This man is so thrilled to go out with you he has no pride.
- He'll take up any hobby you have.
- He'll follow you around if you invite him back to coffee – he's so fascinated by being in a 'girl's place'.
- He'll go overboard on love notes, silly e-mails, and other love tokens.
- He'll show up *early* for dates when you're half-dressed with a facemask on.
- He'll hang all over you if there are any other men around – frightened one will snatch you from under his nose.
- He'll go out of his way to help with things like the DIY around your flat. He's been known to be useful – and then get dumped, poor guy!

The things a 'Mr. Sad & Needy' is most likely to say (usually in a pleading voice):
- 'Why can't you *stay* longer?'
- 'Why can't you *talk* longer?' (on the phone)'
- 'Can't I stay over? I won't be in your way!' And he isn't doing 'a number' on you – he really will leave

you alone but hold on to you all night like a soppy puppy.

🗨️ 'Can I see you again tomorrow?'

🗨️ 'You mean so much to me!' (after the first date)

🗨️ 'You mean everything to me!' (after a couple more)

🗨️ 'I've never enjoyed anyone else's company so much!' Yeah right – like he's had loads of dates – not!

🗨️ And don't forget – he'll be 'in love' with you before you know it!

The reasons he's a frog:

It may seem flattering to have so much attention and affection. After all we complain most men don't give us enough! But it can become annoying really quickly and you'll get fed up with him trying to make your life his!

MR. MISER – 'Me? Spend *my* money on anyone else?'

Signs to watch for:

The frog-like behaviour of a 'Mr. Miser':

❗ He looks uncomfortable when the bill arrives.

❗ Unless he's in the loo when it arrives!

❗ He'll spend loads of time working out the costs of a future date.

❗ He has *no* pride when it comes to his miserly ways.

❗ He carefully counts out money from his wallet – it's a slow process separating himself from it!

❗ He'll always say 'yes' to a freebie (dinner at your friend's, dinner at your mum's, dinner at his mum's!).

❗ He'll have nice, smart clothes – nothing cheap for him!

❗ Don't expect big gorgeous gifts! He'll be cautious

about what he buys you for your birthday or
Christmas.

/ He'll never buy a Big Issue as you two walk down
the road.

/ He'll choose a bargain bottle of wine every time.

The things a 'Mr. Miser' is most likely to say:

👄 'Ooh – that's rather expensive!' When clearly
whatever it is, is not!

👄 As you leave a restaurant – 'That wasn't very good
value!'

👄 'I've had better deals,' referring to anything
bought when out together.

👄 'Do you really want that much?' as you order an
extra course at dinner.

👄 'Waste not, want not,' as he finishes what's on
your plate.

👄 He'll mention the prices of everything he owns –
his house, car, golf clubs (yes, he's likely to have
expensive hobbies himself), etc.

The reasons he's a frog:

This sort of man has usually been single for a long time.
He then gets overly protective of his money and
possessions – and very set in the way he spends money.
Enter you – stage right – into his life and he finds it hard
to break this habit. Generosity in either sex is very
attractive – miserliness is not!

THE BECKHAM-BORE – He's the chap who blends into the sofa because he quite literally lives there following his favourite team, player, etc.

Signs to watch for:

The frog-like behaviour of a 'Beckham':

/ He'll always put the game first even if on your first

date he tries hard not to.

/ You'll find he won't answer the phone when the 'big match' is on even when you know he's there.

/ What are you doing ringing him anyway? Have you learnt nothing?

/ Saturday and Sunday mornings are spent playing his 'sport of choice' to a pathetically low standard.

/ He and the lads then disappear up the pub to pat themselves on the back for their superhuman efforts!

/ You'll only get a look in when there's no big match on, no games to play with the lads, etc.

/ Believe me this is true. I've even dated a 'Beckham-bore'.

/ He'll go out and purchase memorabilia, etc. No money left for dates!

/ He sulks a lot. If his team loses. If you don't show any interest in his sport. Or if you, dare I say it, question how much time he devotes to sport.

/ This man will NOT change – believe me – as he doesn't see it as putting relationships second. He thinks sport is a way of life.

The things a 'Beckham' is most likely to say:

👄 'You don't love . . . (names his favourite sport, team, or player) . . . ?' he says with total disbelief.

👄 As you ask him what time to meet up he'll say, 'Well as soon as the game finishes I'll ring your mobile.'

👄 All sorts of moans, groans, and shouts depending on how the team or player is performing.

👄 His talk will be all sport – he'll always find a way of bringing it into the conversation.

The reasons he's a frog:

This sports mad bloke lives for his 'game' of choice.

There's no way you can compete. And *don't even think* about trying to wean him off his sport. He'll only work as a 'date' if you have a busy life and don't want to see much of someone!

MR. NON-COMMITTER – This man has a phobia of commitment and will only ever settle down when he meets 'Ms. Perfect' – a 'Ms. Possibility' simply won't do.
Signs to watch for:

The frog-like behaviour of a 'Mr. Non-Committer':

- He'll have a track record of many relationships rarely lasting more than a few weeks but perhaps up to three months.
- Just when your dates seem to be going well he'll 'disappear' with no calls, e-mails, or texts for a few days.
- He'll change the conversation when it gets too personal or intimate. He doesn't want you to talk about your family, hopes and dreams – it scares him deep down.
- He won't really want to do things with your friends – or even his. Don't mistake this for 'Mr. Sad & Needy' wanting you all to himself! 'Mr. Non-Committer' simply wants to keep things from getting complicated before he *stops* seeing you.
- If you start sleeping with him (be careful!) he'll freak out if you leave your toothbrush or girly items in his bathroom.
- All his behaviour will point to an independent nature – he won't send loads of texts or e-mails – just enough to keep things ticking over.

The things a 'Mr. Non-Committer' is most likely to say:

- He'll always give you plausible reasons why his 'relationships' haven't worked. Listen carefully and you'll probably identify a pattern. Like all his 'ex-girlfriends' wanted things to get too serious too soon.
- 'I like to take things slowly,' is a favourite phrase.
- 'People seem in such a rush nowadays,' is another.
- He's adept at moving the conversation from personal topics to less threatening territory. When talking about what he's looking for he'll describe a romantic scenario – don't be fooled – this is all a 'Ms. Perfect' fantasy no woman will live up to.
- 'All my friends are getting roped into settling down!' he'll moan.

The reasons he's a frog:

He'll bring you grief. Because basically he's an all right guy and you'll be thinking he'd be a great catch, but believe me something serious will have to happen in his life (trauma or emergency!) before he gets over his phobia of committing. I know you think 'the right love' will bring him around but you're unlikely to succeed.

The serious side of frogs!

Now so far these 'frogs' have seemed fairly tame. Let's move on now to the ones who'll *seriously* break your heart if you're not careful.

THE SERIAL SEDUCER – Mr. dangerous, sex-on-legs, who could charm the knickers off a vicar's wife.

Signs to watch for:

The frog-like behaviour of a 'Serial Seducer':

/ This man will bombard you with texts, e-mails and OTT behaviour that's incredibly flattering but designed with one purpose in mind – to get you into bed.

/ This man will be very touchy-feely and in quite intimate places, too – even on the first date!

/ He'll bring your personal spaces so close that you're practically welded together! OR he'll keep a little distance physically while enticing you *verbally* to move towards him. A ploy to see how vulnerable you are to his 'charms'.

/ He unexpectedly lands up too close. For example, you'll be at the bar ordering your round of drinks and turn to find him breathing down your neck.

/ He's a little too quick to help you on with your coat or out the door with moves that bring him in close contact with you.

/ Generally he'll be of the 'close-encounters when you least expect it' ilk!

/ He seems to eye up his mates' girlfriends – yes he *will* bring you quickly into his circle of friends to give you a false sense of security!

/ He flirts with anyone – your mother, the waitress, the waiter even!

/ Occasionally he'll go on the 'missing list' but not for the same reasons as a non-committer. But because he's bedding someone else!

/ He may act suspiciously when receiving some calls – more likely than not it's another woman ringing.

The things a 'Serial Seducer' is most likely to say:

👄 He'll tell you all the latest blue jokes off the Net.

👄 'You look fantastic,' even when you know you don't. He's too free and easy with the compliments.

🗨 'You are the most exquisite thing!' Yes, serial seducers tend to use OTT adjectives (exquisite) and call women 'things'.

🗨 Any line to get you into bed, particularly things designed to make you feel slightly guilty like, 'I'll burst, you've looked so gorgeous all night!'

🗨 He'll come up with all sorts of outrageous excuses for where he was (when he was supposed to be meeting you). Anything from, 'My dog got off his lead and it took three hours to find him,' to, 'It was terrible – I saw an accident and had to help!'

🗨 And you know he doesn't have a 'good Samaritan' bone in his body!

The reasons he's a frog:

I think this is fairly obvious. This man doesn't want dates, romance and a relationship. He wants high-octane sex and with as many women as possible. You're simply a notch on the bedpost (if you sleep with him against the love doctor's (me!) advice!).

MR. CONTROL FREAK – Being incredibly insecure, but in a more malicious way than 'Mr. Sad & Needy', he'll slowly gain control of what you do, where you go, and worse still – how you feel about yourself!

Signs to watch for:

The frog-like behaviour of a 'Mr. Control Freak':

/ He'll turn up unannounced at your place of work.

/ He'll order your drink and even food off a menu without asking what you'd really like!

/ He'll re-arrange your furniture to his liking.

/ He'll get angry (rather than *hurt* like 'Mr. Sad & Needy') if you make plans with friends without checking with him.

✔ He'll accuse you of flirting with other men when you weren't.
✔ He'll have a 'go' at men who pay interest in you.
✔ He may drink to excess and get morose about his life, or even angrier and more controlling – very scary!

The things a 'Mr. Control Freak' is most likely to say:

💋 'Why do you want to see them tonight?'
💋 'We're never on our own!'
💋 'Your friends don't like me.' Putting the onus on them for being the 'bad guys'.
💋 'I think your hair looks better like this . . .'
💋 'I don't think you should wear *that* . . . try this.'
💋 'Who were you talking to?' when he finds your phone engaged. 'None of your business, mate!' should be your reply!

The reasons he's a frog:
Again I think his behaviour speaks for itself. If it doesn't give you immediate bad vibes you should think of getting counselling. Once in control this man will not let go and can become an obsessive lover.

MR. NASTY – This man is the true misogynist. He simply doesn't like women and will find ways to cause you emotional pain.
Signs to watch for:

The frog-like behaviour of a 'Mr. Nasty':
✔ This man will be less obvious than 'Mr. Control Freak' which makes him all the more dangerous!
✔ He'll set up situations to undermine you. For example he'll arrange to meet you at a designated

time, then show up an hour late claiming you've got the time wrong. You'll go over it in your mind completely sure of how the arrangements were made, but you'll still begin to doubt your sanity.

/ He'll poke fun at you in front of his friends that you've only just met.

/ He'll ignore you at the party he's suggested going to. Or turn his back on you at the pub and talk to someone else.

/ He'll purposely take you to his ex-girlfriend's haunt – hoping to embarrass you both.

The things a 'Mr. Nasty' is most likely to say:

👄 'I'm sure *you've* got the time/place/event wrong.'

👄 'I think women are too forward/masculine/in-your-face nowadays.'

👄 'I'm not sure why we decided to do this!' Or, 'This wasn't a very good idea,' implying he's not enjoying the date.

👄 As your mobile rings he'll sneer, 'Oh God, just typical! A woman who can't stay off the phone for a minute!'

The reasons he's a frog:

Again a 'Mr. Nasty' doesn't need much explaining. Sometimes they're very attractive, successful men and we give them the benefit of the doubt thinking they've simply had a bad day and are grumpy. But that's what they bank on – their date's goodwill! Don't fall for it. If a man acts like this on the first few dates it'll only get worse. Remember most of us put our best foot forward at first. So what's 'Mr. Nasty' going to be like later?!

Other pond life –

Don't forget all sorts of creatures crawl out of ponds – and this is not an exhaustive list! Use your intuition if something's telling you something is wrong with your new date – believe it!

93

DATING SURVIVAL STRATEGY:
Have you ever dated one of the known species
of frogs listed above? YES/NO

If YES – which type?

....

....

What will you do if you come across another frog?

....

....

(Now I'm really hoping you wrote something like 'run a mile!')

The main reason we don't give up on frogs!

Our expectations have a lot to answer for. If we *expect* to treat someone nicely ourselves, then we *expect* the same back. If we give a man a 'chance', and possibly time to get over dating nerves and let their best aspects shine through, or expect to play the dating game fairly, then we expect this in return. But everyone has different expectations. And if you come across a 'frog' (maybe even in camouflage the first couple of dates, so you hope he's a prince) he may expect women to be 'cheats' (that's his past experience), or unreliable, or bossy – and so he reacts to and treats a date *in ways* based on these expectations.

WHAT'S THE DEFINITION OF A PRINCE?

This is the million pound question that depends on many love-factors. Things like what you're looking for in a date at that point in your life. As already mentioned you may want a *bit of bad boy* if you're feeling confident, thriving at work, don't want a man to share your life with and simply want a bit of excitement. Or you may be looking for that 'Mr. P.' to spend the rest of your life with. Only you can know what you're looking for.

But for some general guidance a 'prince' will have the following qualities, attributes and skills:

 He'll make you feel *good* about yourself. And you should already be feeling good about yourself – or trying to!

 He'll do what he says – like ring you and/or meet you when he says. So he's got good old-fashioned reliability.

 He'll flirt but he won't play head games that make you doubt your sanity.

 He'll have a life – i.e. he won't cling to you like a limpet!

 He'll have a sense of fair play about how you two spend your dates. For example, he won't expect you to show up at *his* 'local' at a pre-determined time – like 9.30 p.m. (giving him time with the boys before he sees you!).

 He'll be willing to find out just what satisfies you in terms of foreplay. Yes foreplay! Remember? You're not going *all the way* until the time is right!

 He'll want to know about your life, friends, family, and what makes you tick.

So *go forth* and sort the frogs from the princes! You deserve the best but can take the worst (like 'Serial Seducer') if you like *and* can handle it. I'm not telling you what to do, just how to apply TACTIC SEVEN as most of you will want to go out with the great guys not the second-rate guys!

The most important thing I've learned from TACTIC SEVEN is:

....

....

And I'm not going to forget this!

TACTIC 8:
BE ...

MYSTERIOUS – don't give the game away!

Be honest with me – who would you find more attractive and exciting when *first dating*: 'Male A' – a man who tells you *everything* about himself from his auntie's toileting habits to the last detail of his break-up with his ex. Or 'Male B' – a man who tells you enough to get you interested but won't bore you with the gory details of his father's close relationship with alcohol or the warts he had off his foot – until the time is right. When you want to love him 'warts and all'. Male A is 'Mr. Heart-on-his-sleeve' and Male B is 'Mr. Little-bit-of-mystery'.

I bet 99% of you would fancy Male B more! The man with a bit of camouflage. Funnily enough – men feel the same way about women. They *don't* want to know about your period pains (even when they live with you they probably don't!), or your secret daily journal, or your ex's snoring. They want a bit of excitement, fun, romance and mystery. So keep your camouflage up for the first few weeks, and then *slowly* give him a glimpse here, and a glimpse there, into your life. It's like a striptease – slow and erotic! Not a throw-your-clothes-off and romp in the nude, the first time you meet. Although granted, some men would enjoy that – but for the wrong reasons!

How do you retain mystery?

Mystery is subtle. It's not about playing games – well, if I'm honest it's a *little* about playing games – the game of biding your time and choosing your moments. Beware though that men on the whole *don't* like real game players. It confuses them too much and they do after all need fairly clear signals. But a little bit keeps everyone on their toes in terms of generating 'mystery'. The key is, it's really about *timing* and keeping them wanting to know more about you in every way. The two main ways that people disclose information – and lose mystery – is talking about experiences they've had and events they've faced. And secondly by disclosing their emotions and feelings particularly about the fledgling romance.

EVENTS & EXPERIENCES

We *all* have a history. Some of it sounding quite scary to another person if you *blab it out all at once*. This is key to successfully retaining a sense of mystery. It's best to keep a lid on some aspects of your life until you really trust him. This is also about your rights as a person – no one owes *anyone* new in their life a rundown of their personal history. But too many women feel obliged to 'tell all' – we get the verbal 'runs'. Believing you have no obligation to talk about personal matters will automatically help you to retain some mystery.

So let me illustrate the sort of things you should exercise caution with through the following list:

Events and experiences you should be wary about disclosing too soon or you'll break the mysterious spell you're trying to weave!

/ Avoid all stories about bodily functions (yours in particular!) – I shouldn't have to say more.

/ I've said this before – avoid talking about your ex because it's so easy to slip into delivering a whole dissertation about him. You find the night's gone and so is your 'Mr. P.'. He's assumed you're still hung up on the ex.

/ Avoid the subject of mental illness – yours and any family member's. I've worked in the field of mental health and I think mental health *should* be out there on the table with no shame attached to it! BUT – he won't feel the way I do – and I'm not your date! Men find it tricky to discuss such things unless they've had first hand experience and even then they want time to open up with someone about such experiences.

/ Depression – that's included above even though you may not think so. Men don't know how to react when a woman starts describing her depressive episode that arose from the last time she got dumped. Tell him about the Prozac later on down the line.

/ Avoid at *all costs* talking about your past sexual conquests. Quite frankly you won't impress a man this way. If anything he'll start perceiving you simply as a sh*g.

/ Don't describe hurtful things you've done, e.g., getting an office colleague you didn't like fired, or shredding your ex's clothes for revenge. Such naughty escapades might sound funny (or *not* as the case may be) when describing them to friends over a drink – but he may think you've got a screw loose and run a mile.

/ Telling a date how your parents' divorce left you scarred for life will get him wondering in *what way*. Will you take it out on him? Will you be unable to have a good time? It sets up anxiety he doesn't want to deal with in the early stages of dating.

/ Ill health is another tricky one. So describing the hideous stomach 'flu you had recently where you lost half a stone through 'both ends', is definitely a no-no. Included in this is, e.g., describing the horrible details of when you gave birth. A lot of you will have come out of long-term relationships and/or marriage and want advice for the dating scene – so presumably some will have had children. Medical stories can be great to recount (you survived after all) but not *too* soon.

/ This is an important one. Don't disclose any event or experience relating to traumas like date rape, rape, or abusive relationships until you know he really is interested in you as a *person* – not just you as another potential conquest. Again men find these areas very hard to talk about. They may have lots of empathy for the experience you've had. But they don't know what you want from them when you tell them. A shoulder to cry on? Advice? A shocked response? This makes them feel redundant – or worse – unable to take action (and men like to *do* things, *find* solutions, *be* the saviour, etc.). This immediately sets up the circumstances for failure in your dating. He'll feel negatively (about himself – not you) and NOT want to repeat the experience.

/ Don't put him on the spot by asking about his experience with any of the above! Once he starts 'disclosing', you will too, and then you lose some mystery.

CAUTION ALERT! There are a few absolute 'gems' out there who you couldn't shock even with the worst stories of a turbulent past. But unless *you* can identify him as a gem, you should proceed with caution talking about subjects like those above until you feel you've established trust and your dates are turning into a relationship. It's not that I think men should run from such topics but I know from talking to hundreds (thousands even!) of men that they get scared, worried and don't know what to say – the poor souls!

EMOTIONS

Keeping your emotions a bit of a mystery will enhance your *desirability*. Unlike your girlfriends who want to hear every detail of the way you *felt* when x, y, or z happened, a man does not – at least early on. So what am I talking about?

- Avoid the 'L' word – 'like' or 'love' – until you two are really comfortable. Let it get to the point in your dating that he's *wondering* how you feel. Make him sweat. Men are so used to women announcing this earlier than they would. So you have to be *different*. Different makes you mysterious. There's nothing worse than announcing you 'love him' when he's not ready to hear it. I'll let you in on something. I once mortified myself doing this to the man who did become my second (and present) husband. But it was touch and go after blurting out, 'I love you' when we'd been seeing each other six weeks. He'd been kissing me goodnight on my doorstep and it just came out. He stammered (and he doesn't usually!) something like, 'I like you'. You can imagine how I felt. Like a complete plonker! But even the love doctor is allowed some mistakes

– now I can share this with you. I think you should try and coax it out of him if you're ready to hear it. You can snuggle up and say something like, 'Things are good, aren't they?' Not too threatening. Not too emotional. So hold back and wait for his 'I'm-in-love' cues probably between the two and three month mark but it may be longer. Some men find it very hard to ever say it. But if they're *showing* you love with loving behaviour, then that's a good thing.

/ Don't let them know you've been having mood swings over stress at work, that time of the month, or even coming out and meeting him. Men don't like things getting too emotional *too soon* in terms of knowing about the inner workings of your feelings. Just keep your emotions in check when around him.

/ Don't go OTT telling him how 'awful' something was at work, how heartbroken you were over a soppy movie, etc. The more you drag big emotions into the conversation on the first few dates – the more edgy he'll feel. And the more he'll know about the side of you that you want to keep a mystery! Also back to that old chestnut – you want him to feel *good* around you – not wondering if you're on the verge of tears!

/ Again, as with the last list respect his 'mystery' – don't try dragging his emotions out of him! He won't like it and again you jeopardise how he feels towards you.

Some simple truths to keep you camouflaged until he's captured!

Aside from events and experiences and disclosing your emotions, here are a few pointers to keep him guessing:

⭐ If he's got plans – so have you! It always happens. You've met someone new and they have tickets to something with friends for a great evening out, but the event is sold out and it's impossible to get you a ticket to join them (this was of course booked before you two met). He says something like, 'I hate to think of you sitting in when I'm at this exciting event.' You have to be quick with the response. 'Don't worry, I've got plans already that night. So it works out fine!' Then don't tell him what your plans are. It's a mystery, remember!

⭐ When he rings don't blurt out that you were just washing your hair. Simply don't say anything. He'll wonder what he interrupted and if he asks, keep it simple like you were just getting ready to go out or ring someone back who'd left a message. This sounds intriguing like washing hair never will!

⭐ Having male friends is great – and they can come in handy when you're first dating. For example, 'Mr. P.' has come back for coffee and one of your male friends rings. You can say very loudly, 'Hi, Dave! How lovely to hear from you!'. As you come off the phone *don't* explain who Dave is. This is not playing a game it's simply you minding your business! But if 'Mr. P.' asks you know he's interested. You can answer simply, 'Oh Dave? He's just a good friend.' You *don't* want to generate insane jealousy but rather interest in the male friends you may have.

⭐ Equally part of your mystery will be NOT to ask him about such phone calls he receives! Because that'll really get him thinking, 'how much does she like me?' creating incentive for him to crank up 'the chase'. Yes, men are that bad – if they like you but don't think you're infatuated with them – they'll want you even more!

★ As mentioned earlier in TACTIC FIVE don't be available to talk on the phone for ages. Remember you're a *busy*, desirable woman. No matter how much you fancy him you can't let him know at first. Saying, 'Oh I'm going to have to cut this conversation short,' without saying why, will have him intrigued. You want that!

★ Space your dates even if you're dying to see him and all your friends are too broke to go out. It's important to keep the mystery of your social diary alive and thriving. Don't tell him where you go, who you're going with, and for how long – that's for married couples. This really drives men nuts – believe me – they tell me.

★ Small things like not letting on how much time it takes you to get ready for a date can help keep him interested. If you describe in detail that it took you 30 minutes to do your facemask and eyebrow shaping, another 20 to blow-dry your hair, then 15 more to apply some make-up, he'll be reeling with boredom! Some things need to be a mystery. While we're on minor personal habits he also doesn't need to know if you've had to erect some sort of bra-like mechanism to keep your modesty intact for the particular dress you're wearing. Or that you've got clear nail varnish keeping the holes in your tights from laddering, etc. Just let him marvel at how beautiful the finished product is!

★ Your ex may come in handy for creating a little bit of mystery (I just *knew* an ex has a purpose!). Let's just say you and your ex have to be in contact – maybe over children, money, selling a property, etc. Well, slip into the conversation that you've been dealing with your ex. If he asks, 'Does your ex want you back?' be enigmatic by saying something like, 'I'm not sure . . . but I'm not interested.' You won't be lying per se. Maybe your ex is *still* interested – who knows. But it'll definitely enhance your social value to be a little vague. Why do you think the famous painting by Leonardo da Vinci, the Mona Lisa, has captured the attention of millions throughout the centuries? Because we can't quite fathom out her enigmatic smile. Think about that!

★ Exaggeration can get you everywhere! Let's just say there's a man at work who flirts with you a little. You know this colleague really doesn't want to take you out but occasionally you two share a pleasant 'flirt moment'. Well it won't hurt if you nonchalantly drop into the conversation how much this guy at work is *always* trying to flirt with you. Again this'll make you seem desirable with only a touch of 'embroidery' – and does that really hurt in the jungle of love? Again, exercise caution because if you go too far you'll generate too much of that very difficult emotion – jealousy. Too much is too challenging to a man. If you've got a big conscience and a need for complete honesty – once you two are in love, and in couple-dom, you can own up to any little tricks and ploys you used to create some mystery in the early stages of dating.

For the future:

Even once you've captured him and got him out of the dating jungle some things should always stay a mystery if you want to keep your love alive. These include:

/ Going to the loo – this should be private. Keeping smells at bay is important to lasting love – this just isn't sexy. Let him think you always smell of roses!

/ Looking your absolute worst should be reserved for emergencies only – like the stomach 'flu. Otherwise running a brush through your hair occasionally – just to be presentable – will make you feel good and him adore you.

/ Illness is a tricky subject. If you really *need* him in a time of illness – he'll have to help you, e.g., to the A & E for treatment. But it's better to keep things like the stomach 'flu behind closed doors. It never hurts to retain a little mystery. You don't want to see what he chucks up with the stomach 'flu – so will he want to see your stomach contents?

/ Events like plucking your nose or nipple hairs should be kept a mystery. Lots of women have these but men think women don't. Why should they know any different? So don't blow this mystery for the rest of women! Again you don't want to see him tweeze his nose hairs so . . . Teeth flossing, ear cleaning, etc. These should all go in the same 'behind-closed-doors, what's-she-doing-in-there?' mystery. Keep him wondering!

The above may sound old-fashioned to some – but, hey, in decades past they didn't have the vast divorce and relationship break-down rate we have now. And they certainly kept things a bit more private! So maybe they had something there. Retaining a little mystery and dignity will definitely smooth the path of your new love and keep it flowing!

The most important thing I've learned from TACTIC EIGHT is:

....
....

And I'm not going to forget this!

TACTIC 9:
BE ...

A BIT OF A B**** – in the nicest possible way!

This TACTIC is going to be short and sweet – but you *won't* be! In all my years as a psychologist, agony aunt and life coach, I can say the one thing *most* women do wrong is be *too* nice! We are taught from our earliest days to 'nurture' others, bend over backwards to please people, and generally put ourselves *second*. Well, in the jungle that is the dating scene – not only does this need to be balanced out, but also *reversed* at times. You have to go further than simply expecting to be an 'equal' to your date. You have to be a bit of a b*tch!

All the TACTICS so far have been about finding balance in the way you use and develop your dating skills – so you don't go over the top in either direction. Either trying to be an in-your-face, new 'ladette' (that'll intimidate him *or* he won't take you seriously) or acting like a shrinking violet (and as it's the survival of the fittest out there – you won't be fit for dating!). It's been about having your own life, being confident, but also being aware of how a man thinks and feels – and views you!

But there are times when you just simply have to assert yourself *more*, maybe even surprising him by putting him in his place a bit, and putting yourself first.

Just how am I going to get many of you (being typical, overly nice women) to incorporate these, what men might view as bitchy, attitudes – when needed – to get the most out of dating? My simple and cunning plan is to list the key elements to being *successfully* bitchy (think Mae West – now she was no shrinking violet and yet men found her irresistible! She'd put a guy in his place without him even knowing).

The situations where your newfound bitchiness is essential:

★ **Male Pressure to Have Sex!** Some of the men you date will immediately try to get the upper hand by applying enormous pressure to have sex. This is a no-no – he should not be doing this! And he may well be the sort of guy you stop seeing straight away. Or he may be the sort who once put in his place, is O.K. So what's your response? Do you get all *embarrassed*, feel *guilty* that somehow maybe he's right (you should have sex), is your confidence *shaken*? No, your attitude is 'in your dreams, mate!' So when responding to such pressure simply let him know in no uncertain terms that he's got a long wait – and it'll be even longer if he keeps the pressure up! Men who try it on to this extent need strong comebacks that may appear bitchy, but in the long run they work.

★ **When Dumping!** It's actually best for a man to be dumped speedily and ruthlessly. Because if he's *really* interested in you, he may *not* be telling you at this stage of the game, secretly clinging to a lot of hope that it'll work out. In these circumstances he's in a heightened state of winning the 'chase'.

He is totally goal-focused and *you* are his goal. If you've decided after the first few dates, or weeks even, that you don't want to continue this fledgling romance, you have to be ruthlessly straightforward.

If, like most overly nice women, you worry about letting him down gently he simply *won't* get it. He may think you're playing hard to get. Or he may think as long as there's *one chance* in a million of success – he'll keep at it – he's in 'chase mode' after all! So look him straight in the eye and tell him there'll be no more dates.

⭐ **Explanations!** When dumping there are two elements for consideration as to *how far* you take your explanation. If it's something he *can* change (e.g. bellowing bawdy jokes at the top of his voice in the middle of a bar so everyone else hears and you're mortified; ringing his mum to check in with her about his plans (fine at 15, not at 25!); burping/farting and thinking it's funny/clever – he never got past the 13 year old boy stage of maturity) you should be absolutely honest about it and tell him. Sounds really bitchy, huh? No! It's actually bitchier to let him carry on annoying women and losing them, when he could actually turn things around for himself.

If, however, it's something he can't change (e.g. his rather large nose that you initially thought gave him 'character' but now puts you right off kissing him; his job – that he loves and talks about continually – but you find quite frankly boring; his height that didn't bother you at first but actually drives you mad as even in 'flats' you're still two inches taller) then you have to go easy. He can't after all get a nose job, change his job, or take growth hormones for you, can he? So give him a believable excuse but still deliver it as if you mean it! 'I'm too busy at work to date right now,' is a handy one.

⭐ **Girlfriends First!** A man never quite fathoms what it is that makes our friendships so special. Quite frankly a lot feel they don't even want to *go there*. It's really important that you keep connected with your girlfriends – they're forever but men come and go. And ensure he knows the value you place on them. He should know you've got 'dates' with them to keep and that you won't break them. Because you're likely to get pressure over this issue. So many women write to me in my agony aunt 'hat' saying, 'My best friend's deserted me for her new man!' Often it's a mixture of male pressure and their own hormones making them forget the importance of friends.

If for example, a girlfriend rings you on your mobile during a date, don't whisper to her in hurried tones, 'Can't talk – gotta go!' Instead give her a few minutes – this'll really throw him – he'll expect to be 'king bee'. Actually it sends a powerful message – don't mess with my friendships. An *overly nice* and typical response is, 'I'm sorry – she does go on a bit.' But you're not going to do that! This doesn't mean you're creating warfare between him and her – you're simply marking your boundaries and they're not to be messed with.

⭐ **Your Clothes!** If he ever suggests anything about your choice of clothes – stand your ground. In the first place men use clothes as a means of starting to control a woman – a bad thing. They do this by controlling, e.g., the level of sexiness of clothes they *approve* of usually to one extreme or the other. They may want you to 'look more sexy' to show you off to friends (like a prized pet), or they may hate it if you look too sexy as they feel threatened by other men looking at you.

The only exception is if you've asked the all time girly-est question – 'does my bum look big in this?' and he replies that if you're worried you should change! Well, you brought that on yourself! Or if he's invited you to an event and you ask him for guidelines – that's fine.

⭐ Stick up for your beliefs! There are always dating situations where we're made to feel uncomfortable and we 'laugh them off' only to kick ourselves later for not being honest with our date. We laugh these things off because we're too nice to say what we think or how we feel at the time. The sort of things I'm talking about are when your date makes a sexist remark, or tells an offensive joke, or ridicules the waiter's service unnecessarily. To keep the 'peace' you grin a little and try to change the subject – particularly if you like him. But that's not good enough – *especially* if you like him! Saying what you think in a very clear way in such moments will prevent these moments from arising in future. And if you like him, that gives it a better chance for your young romance to succeed. Because hopefully if you pull him up short he'll take notice and know you don't like the sort of thing he did.

DATING SURVIVAL STRATEGY: ARE YOU OVERLY NICE AND AN UNLIKELY B*TCH?
Do you recognise any of the above scenarios?   YES/NO

What were the circumstances?

....
....

Could you have applied any of the suggestions above?

....

....

A final thought on your newfound skills of bitchiness!

As always my list can't be exclusive. You need to use your judgement as situations arise. Perhaps where you feel you have to stand your ground, give your opinion, stick up for yourself or put him in his place *firmly*. Being a bit of a b*tch will have tremendous payoffs, but this is quite different from becoming a total b*tch – now that really will stop you *surviving* dating experiences!

The most important thing I've learned from TACTIC NINE is:

....

....

And I'm not going to forget this!

TACTIC 10:
BE ...

AWARE of dating blind spots!

So you've been exploring the jungle of love for a while now. You've started (hopefully!) to employ my TACTICS for total success. And now you need to ensure you don't sabotage yourself by stumbling into a dating 'blind spot'. If, as the saying goes, *love is blind*, then dating is blind as well as being completely delusional. We sometimes delude ourselves into thinking we're coming across well (you know, confident, desirable, interesting company even!) on a date – when actually the man can't wait for it to be over. We delude ourselves that someone *is* interested – when they're *not*. Or *not* interested – when they *are*! We get things wrong in many ways – otherwise the path of love would run smoothly, wouldn't it!

The following is a list of typical blind spots – to help smooth your path. A sort of odds and ends (or bin ends!) of things you ought to consider before plunging further into the jungle. These are the final things to ensure you survive and enjoy your dating encounters.

⭐ **When *he* doesn't want to go out with *you*! (Obviously he has NO taste!) –**

Let's deal with this most painful scenario first. I've said it before and I'll say it again – men are terrible about being honest when they're *not interested*. Picture this – the first couple of dates went well from your point of view. You're looking forward to another and then he rings to say there won't be one. (At least this guy has rung!)

When you ask 'why' he manages to come up with one of the following rather lame excuses:

Excuse	*What he really means*
'You're too good for me'	'I'm too good for you'
'I'm just not looking for a relationship right now'	'At least not with you'
'If only we'd met at another time'	'You just don't do it for me'
'It's too soon after my ex'	'I'm still in love with her – you don't match up'

So unfortunately you can rarely believe the excuses he'll give you. And if you can't work it out – move on and don't waste your energy.

⭐ **When he *does* want to go out with you! (Body Language to look out for)**

A quick reminder of the Body Language tips from TACTIC TWO, to ensure you are not 'blind' to a potential great mate!

'Mr. P.s' Body Language –

1. Watch out for him doing 'The Bridge', 'The Twist', 'The Slide' or 'The Screen', as men use these pieces of body language too.

2. Men will draw your eye downwards to their hips (yes, this *is* suggestive!) by looping a finger or thumb in their belt loop.

3. 'The Throat Clear' – When about to say something that subconsciously is getting on personal territory (showing more than likely they're interested) many men will do a brief throat clear. This gives them a moment to build confidence to tackle this area. For example, if they want to find out how recently you had a relationship.

4. Watch out for 'The Saunter' – this is that male way of swaggering when they either fancy you (great!) or think they're on to an *easy thing* (what message have you been giving off girl?)

5. If as the evening progresses he seems to use a whole body 'Screen', then he's really interested. This is more than a shoulder 'Screen' – his subconscious wants to protect you from the attention of others – the competition.

6. When walking together (to your table, etc.) if he 'Bridges' to either your arm or your lower back he again is positively interested.

7. Men and their hair presents a slightly different picture from women and their hair. A long stroke suggest he's interested. But a 'flick' suggests he's impatient.

8. Lingering looks – you know when you feel a man's assessing your potential – the way they can look you up and down. Well, they *are* assessing your potential. And they're not being completely shallow looking at your physical attributes – they

also pick up your body language cues. So if he gives you the once-over more than once during the date he's fine-tuning his overall first impression – that's a good sign! You're winning the battle. Unless of course as the date's worn on *you've* lost interest.

 RULE OF THREE

Please don't confuse this with the 'rule of three' mentioned in the movie hit 'American Pie II'. In this movie whatever number of conquests a man *said* he had, you were to divide by three to get the real number. Men upsize for their egos! And with a woman you were supposed to multiply by three – as women tend to 'downsize' their number of lovers. My 'rule of three' is about prevention – of losing him if you like him at the critical hurdles of the 'third date', 'three weeks of dating', and the 'three month hurdle'.

Three dates – It's by the third date we decide whether there is – or is not – an immediate passion or interest enough to keep seeing the person. Of course at first impressions on the first date we've decided there's some sort of interest. But three dates can make or break the situation and is often the point where he never rings again. So treat date no. 3 like the first – be on your best if you like him and you'll pass this hurdle. Also don't fall for the trap that you've got to have sex on the third date – this just is not the case. You have sex when you're confident about the reasons for it and feel in control.

Three weeks – It's at the three-week mark that irritating habits start to rear their ugly little heads. If there's only *half-hearted* interest in the romance by this point then people make their excuses and bow out. If there's *real* interest then you'll probably accept these things and hang in there.

Three months – The power struggles start around this point. Often based around the need to hear three magic words, 'I love you' or 'let's move in'. Usually (but not always) this pressure comes from the woman. If the man doesn't rise to the occasion by taking the relationship to the next level a variety of problems may set in. Rows start, communication is blocked, and feelings are hurt. It's make or break time to go to another level. Keep calm. Remember he may not feel happy articulating the depth of his feelings – even if they're strong. Talk clearly and don't turn such things into rows. It's critical to build the trust at this stage that feelings can be spoken about honestly. And without risk to his nerves at this stage!

If you make it past the three-month hurdle then at some point the tricky issue of 'commitment' will raise its head. There is no hard and fast rule about when people should move in, marry, or become completely exclusive and committed emotionally and sexually. The individual chemistry and circumstances between two people vary tremendously. For some they may get engaged at three months. For others it may be three years. And of course for many, commitment means co-habiting rather than marriage. However, generally speaking research shows that those who meet, date and then 'commit' (marry or co-habit) during the one to two-and-a-half year time frame are more likely to have lasting relationships.

Those who commit before one year may actually be playing out insecurities that eventually lead to their downfall. Those who commit after two and a half years may secretly find commitment hard and in some sense go in to it grudgingly. Beware though that co-habiting relationships fall apart at a much higher rate than marriages.

At the end of the day, after dating for a period of time, you have to balance your desire to commit with his. If it causes disagreements, do some heart searching about whether your expectations, or his, are unreasonable or his, or in fact whether they're compatible at all. It sometimes hurts to leave a relationship, e.g., if one of you doesn't want to marry. But if you desire the whole works – marriage, home, children, etc., you'd be advised to think carefully about compromising these.

★ WHY MEN DON'T RING WHEN THEY SAY THEY WILL

Women have a real blind spot about this issue when in actual fact it's quite simple.

There are two main explanations why men take our numbers and then don't ring. The first and least painful is the simple fact they managed to be brave enough to take it but they now are worried about rejection so don't *use* it. How frustrating for us is that? Because we then think of at least ten reasons why they didn't really fancy us. The second and harsh reason is quite simply that they used taking your number as a ploy to leave the situation. They weren't interested but it seemed easier to say, 'I'll ring you,' than to say, 'you won't be getting a call from me, mate!'

So stop fretting that he was knocked over by a car – so can't ring. Or that the bit of paper your number was on was swept away in a hurricane, etc. These things happen in movies! Don't wait (i.e. don't be a 'princess'!) but move on to the next. The biggest predictor of whether or not he'll use your number is what he says when he takes it. If he says, 'I'll give you a call sometime' – that's a bad sign. If on the other hand he says, 'I'll call you tomorrow,' or, 'Tuesday', or 'this week', – that's a good sign. He's actually pinning down taking your number and using it to a time frame. But it still doesn't guarantee he won't get nerves and *fail* to call.

★ THE STEREOTYPE TRAP

It's very easy to stereotype men too quickly. We don't like it when they do this to us and it's the same for them. Unfortunately it's human nature to stereotype. We come across so many people during our daily life and have to make rapid judgements about them and their motivation, but a lot of great guys are missed this way. We judge them because of their style of dress (or lack of it), because they're not tall enough, or cute enough. But people can grow on us given half the chance. So beware of this common blind spot. You'll overlook many good ones on the trail to happiness. Try to be more open-minded and not to make snap judgements.

★ LET ME INTRODUCE HIS SUBCONSCIOUS TO YOURS

Sometimes we have an inexplicable and rapid attraction to someone and we can't fathom out why. This is the meeting of your subconscious with his. Our subconscious minds 'speak' to each other. We pick up very subtle clues about a person's background and personality. You know this is happening when you get a sense that 'you've known each other forever'. Run with these feelings, as often they're good indicators of compatibility, while keeping your conscious mind alert to using the TEN TACTICS.

⭐ MISSED CHANCES

Hundreds, maybe thousands, of women have complained to me over the years about missing chances. Let's say you're out with your best friend and you spot some good-looking guy who hasn't spotted you yet. You hum and hah about what to do. Your girlfriend eggs you on to at least walk past him and smile. But in the end you chicken out. Why? Because you're afraid of rejection or looking desperate? Let me assure you now that most men would absolutely love you to say 'hello' or get their attention and smile. So don't whine to me about this blind spot. Be quicker off the mark next time. And once you've grabbed his attention then you can let him make the next move – if he's interested he will. The early bird catches the worm, remember!

⭐ GET A GRIP!

There's a romantic urban myth that too many women buy into and it becomes a blind spot. This one says you should be looking for 'love at first sight'. This sets up all sorts of expectations for that first date that are nearly impossible to live up to. When you're hoping it'll be 'love at first date' you'll send out a vibe that shouts – 'I wonder if you're going to be the *one*?' Most men run a mile from that. And I think that vibe has a lot to do with men saying after the first date, 'I'll call you,' (as above) and then they don't. Getting a grip means going on dates for some fun. To get to know someone new. To do something different. Then you stand a better chance of it going well – and hopefully leading to more.

Debbie is a good example of this. She kept missing out on some great guys because she believed if she didn't feel it was love at first sight then he couldn't be *special enough*. Her friends were exasperated by the fact she'd totally fallen for this myth. They'd all been there to some extent – hoping they'd know the moment 'Mr. P.' came into their sights. But Debbie had gone to extremes and simply didn't give men a chance.

Once we worked on opening up her *expectations* to simply have fun and a bit of romance – then she met someone who grew on her after a few dates. At first he was just fun – then she really began to fancy him. So if you go in expecting 'fun at first date', you're more likely to find love.

★ WHO PAYS?

This is the million £ question that single people make too big a deal of. There's a simple answer to this though. You have to be honest about *your expectations* and do what you feel *comfortable* with. And make this *clear to him*! You have to know what feels right – then believe in it and act on it. Lots of different things will feel right to different women. Some women will expect that whoever did the asking out (him or her), does the paying. Others will expect that bills should always be shared. And some of you will be old-fashioned girls who think the guy should pick up the bill (believe me particularly in the 'Bridget Jones' age group, the 28 to 39 year olds reading this, plenty will feel this way). As long as you don't feel obliged to be dessert! All of these are fine. You simply have to be straight with him about it.

Let's say, for example, you're an old-fashioned girl and really believe he should pay when he takes you out. You'll simply end up resenting him if he says, 'What do you want to do about the bill?' (he *may* be happy to pay it but is simply sounding you out) and you don't have the nerve to tell him. So be clear and honest. The clearer you are in saying e.g., 'I really think the man should pay,' or 'We should split the bill,' the happier he'll be. Men hate awkward money-moments, taking it as a reflection on their manliness. 'Oh, this is awkward – she thinks I can't even sort out a bill!' Yes, they are as insecure as we are!

⭐ INTERNET, AGENCY AND PERSONAL COLUMN DATING

All the mod cons at our disposal nowadays mean that you may find dates in all sorts of ways. Traditional ways – like a friend setting you up or dating agencies (with their video clips in which you sell yourself), phone chat lines, the internet chat rooms and internet dating services. All these are fine because when you come face to face with your date, you'll still need to apply my TACTICS.

As I mentioned in TACTIC TWO, though, you *always* need to use common sense when dating someone new in terms of your safety. So at the risk of repeating myself – but this is so important as you need to be aware – follow a few guidelines to keep yourself safe:

> Always let someone know where you're going, who you're meeting and when to expect you home.
> Always meet someone in a public place.
> Never go home with them, or invite them to yours on first meeting.
> Keep your mobile on.
> Carry a 'siren whistle' to use if they turn out

not to be the person you'd hoped.

It's best to give only your mobile number and not your home phone number until you know them better.

Take their number and dial '141' before calling them, so they can't trace yours.

⭐ DATES FROM HELL

Everyone has a 'date from hell' story to tell. The important thing is NOT to let a date from hell (DFH) knock your confidence. Instead use it as a learning experience! My DFH happened a year after my divorce in 1993. A friend of mine kept telling me I must have a date with a friend of his. This guy looked like George Clooney and not only had a successful business but came from moneyed stock *and* was in the Cosmo most eligible bachelors list.

Well, seeing as George Clooney is my idea of heaven I couldn't wait for the date. This man, who'll remain nameless, and I had met briefly once at my friend's. So I knew he really did look like George. The evening arrived and we chose a local restaurant to have a drink and dinner. This was about two weeks before Christmas (why this is relevant you'll soon see!). We chatted for about ten minutes over a glass of wine when he clasped my hand, looked me straight in the eye and said (quite seriously) – 'You and I will be in bed before Christmas.' I was gob-smacked. Not only would I NOT have been thinking that but I was affronted by his assumption that I just might be a 'desperate divorcee'. I removed my hand from his evil grasp (just kidding – he wasn't evil, simply bad mannered and full of himself!) and looked him back in the eye saying, 'No – I don't think so.' I then finished my drink and said dinner was off and went home. Some may not think this was a DFH but it was! I'd had high hopes (mistake – just think 'fun'!) as he *sounded* so suitable for romance. But sounding it and being it, is another thing.

Just make sure you're never a DFH. It can go both ways!

And finally –

Dating can be lots of fun – *pure bliss* even. A new man you really like can quite literally take your breath away. Finding the person who makes you happy and you can fall in love with is a wonderful thing. And that's how I'd like it to be for you. But remember, along the way you'll be challenged! You may think a man is *perfect* for you – but he doesn't feel the same about you. So you'll have to kick start your dating confidence (TACTIC THREE). You'll come across some frogs that make you doubt your judgement (TACTIC SEVEN). You may be tempted to dive into bed with a Brad Pitt look-alike – even though he shows all the signs of being a womaniser (TACTIC FOUR). You may find it hard to resist showing a man you know-it-all about something (TACTIC SIX). You may find yourself sitting around waiting for that new Mr. P.'s phone call (TACTIC FIVE). And more. These are not failures they are learning experiences! When these things happen remind yourself to continue to put my TEN TACTICS to work for your total success. It's a jungle out there and these will help you survive – even better they'll help you *thrive*! Good luck and happy hunting.

The most important thing I've learned from TACTIC TEN is:

....

....

And I'm not going to forget this!